About the Author

After working on the frontline during the pandemic and after I caught COVID and ended up with long COVID, I spent every minute in pain due to my symptoms. I found escape in writing; I could create a world and escape into it.

The FA Cup

William MacDonald

The FA Cup

Olympia Publishers
London

www.olympiapublishers.com
OLYMPIA PAPERBACK EDITION

A CIP catalogue record for this title is
available from the British Library.

ISBN: 978-1-80439-121-1

This is a work of fiction.
Names, characters, places and incidents originate from the writer's
imagination. Any resemblance to actual persons, living or dead, is
purely coincidental.

First Published in 2023

Olympia Publishers
Tallis House
2 Tallis Street
London
EC4Y 0AB

Printed in Great Britain

Dedication

I dedicate this book to my wife, Emma MacDonald, and to all the frontline workers during the pandemic.

Acknowledgements

A Special thanks to B@M Care who have supported and offered me counsel in my suffering from long COVID.

Chapter 1

The Will

"He is running down the wing, he is one on with the Keeper we are in eighty-eight Minute of the World cup final and Logan is steaming down the wing. Oh no and hands has just come steam rolled through Logan has just gone flying through the air and Logan is crumble pile on the floor—the medical team is surrounding Logan." The television is paused and then it rewound. "He is running down the wing, he is one on with the keeper we are in eighty-eighth minute of the World Cup final and Logan is steaming down the wing. Oh no and Hands has just steam rolled through, Logan has just gone flying through the air and Logan is in a crumbled pile on the floor the medical team is surrounding Logan." The television is paused and then rewound. "He is running down the wing he is one on with the keeper we are in eighty-eighth minute of the World Cup final and Logan is steaming down the wing. Oh no and Hands has just steam rolled through, Logan has just gone flying through the air and Logan is in a crumbled pile on the floor the medical team surrounding Logan". The television is again paused and again rewound. "He is running down the wing he is one on with the keeper we are in eighty-eighth minute of the World Cup final and Logan is steaming down the wing. Oh no and Hands has just steam rolled through,

Logan has just gone flying through the air and Logan is in a crumbled pile on the floor the medical team surrounding Logan". The phone starts to ring, he pulls himself up from the chair moving the pile of beer cans and take away boxes, he lifted the handset of the phone and said in a deep, hungover voice, "Hello, who's there?" The voice on the other end of the phone was a deep husky aged voice. "Hello is this Howard Logan?"

Logan replied with, "It depends who is asking."

Replied, "I am calling from Smith and Smith. We are the firm who-are looking after your uncle's affairs and he has—

"Before he could carry on Logan said, "Hold on, what has happened to my uncle?"

Then the voice said, "I'm sorry to inform you that your uncle was in car accident and tragically lost his life. In his will he has left you his house and his bar in Dorkchester. I believe that this is your hometown, you just need to come to the office and sign the paperwork and we will hand over the keys and deeds to the bar and it is all yours. When can you come into the office?"

"I can come into the office on Tuesday," he replied.

The other voice then said, "We shall see you Tuesday." Logan then put the phone down and again walked through the beer cans and take-away boxes. Logan sat back in his chair and lifted up the remote and then pressed play. "He is running down the wing he is one on with the keeper we are in eighty-eighth minute of the World Cup final and Logan is steaming down the wing. Oh no and Hands has just steam rolled through, Logan has just gone flying through the air and Logan is in a crumpled pile on the floor the medical team are surrounding Logan.

Tuesday had arrived. Logan walked into the Smith and Smith office and took the elevator up to the fifth floor. He saw a desk and there was a blonde lady sitting there. Logan walked over to the desk, as he got closer to the desk he could see the blonde girl was wearing a red dress. She was typing away at the computer. She looked up and saw Logan standing there, "Hello," she said in very low voice.

Logan, with his gruff voice replied, "My name is Logan I have a meeting with Smith and Smith," The young lady pressed a button on her desk and said over her intercom "Mr Logan is here," The reply that came from the intercom was "send him in, we are ready for him." The blonde girl looked at Logan and said "They are ready for you." Logan turned but just as he did he gave the blonde girl a wink and walked through the double doors. He then saw two elderly gentlemen standing over a desk with papers spread out all over them he walked over to the gentleman. They looked over at him and the gentleman to the left said "Good afternoon Mr Logan. Welcome we have the papers for you to sign." Logan looked at the gentleman and he said "Hold on before we sign anything and I agree to anything, I just have a few questions. Why would my uncle give me his house and his bar? I haven't seen my uncle in over twenty years, not since I was signed for Chelsea as a schoolboy and we moved to London and what am I meant to do with a bar in Dorkchester? I have my apartment in London," The second Gentleman with a gentle voice said "We are just following your uncle's will and in this he has left you his house and his bar."

Logan in a raised voice said "Where is this will? I want to see for myself to what it says."

The gentleman to the left passes Logan a piece of paper. Logan then looks at the paper:

This is the last will and testament of Stanley David Logan I leave all my remaining wealth to Dementia UK. I have no children of my own so I leave my house 32 Smith Street to my only nephew, Howard I also have a stake in the Dorkchester FC

13

which I also give to my nephew. I hope that my Nephew can continue to help the bar and the team continue to thrive and be a part of the town of Dorkchester. My nephew has had a hard time lately and by being part of something new, maybe he can find himself again Yours sincerely Stanley David Logan.

Logan threw the piece of paper away and in a raised voice said "This is ridiculous. Why would he leave me this. Our Families haven't spoken in years and I haven't been home to Dorkchester for twenty years. When I was eight I was signed by Chelsea to their youth team and never looked back. We moved to London and we never looked back or even thought about Boring old Dorkchester I have my life in London I am not moving back to Dorkchester ever." So you can keep the keys."

"I'm sorry Mr Logan but the keys are yours. Why don't you take a trip to Dorkchester and speak to the Housing agent and put the property up for sale and then you can return to your life in London and never have to worry about the town of Dorchester again." The gentleman to the left reply to him. Logan grabbed a pen off the table and in a high raised voice said "Let's get on with this then." The gentleman to the right then walk to the table and put the papers onto the table and asked Logan, "You need to sign here and here and finally here," pointing to places on the paper. Logan took the papers and signed on the line. He saw that was a loose bit paper on the table, he took the pen and wrote down on the bit paper and he then folded the piece of paper and folded his hand he then clenched his hand holding the piece of paper. The gentleman to the left walked over to Logan and handed him a set of keys and he held out his hand to shake Logan's hand. Logan then looked at the Gentleman and said "I guess that is all then."

Logan turned and walked out the door, as he passed the desk of the blond girl. he took the peice of the paper and dropped it

14

onto the desk and walked out of the office of Smith and Smith.

The Blonde girl opened up the piece of paper; it said 'Call me 079223344 and make sure you bring the red dress.'

Bang! Bang! Bang! Logan was woken up by banging at his front door. He rolled over, next to him in his bed was the blonde girl from Smith and Smith. Logan rolled out of bed and he walked over to his door. On the floor was the red dress and next to it were a pair of red thong knickers. He opened up the door and there were two men standing in the doorway in dark black trousers and white shirts, with black jackets. One of them was short and bald and second was tall and built like he went to the gym regularly. The bald gentleman said "We are high court enforcement agents and we are here to take control of this property."

Logan looked at him and said "what?" The tall gentleman then replied to him "We are here to take control of the property due to unpaid rent. You can collect some essential belongings and then you can make arrangements with us to collect the rest of your stuff but you must vacate this property today. If you would kindly put on some clothes and collect what you need we can change the locks and carry on with what we need to do."

Logan was pacing up and down, still naked and was getting angry and in a very high raised voice replied "What do you mean? I know that I was behind with a few payments but I have not seen any letters to say that they were going to kick me out."

The bald gentleman then said "Unfortunately, as it was taken to the high court we have a writ of possession you would have letters to say that it had been taken to the high courts." Logan looked over to a table that was in the far left corner of his apartment there was big pile of letters that had not been opened. Logan turned around and showing his bare naked bare arse to the gentleman he also noticed that the blonde lady was slipping on her dress and she was grabbing her shoes. She walked over to Logan and kissed him on the cheeks before walking out his front door. Logan walked over to his bed and he noticed that the red thong was still on the floor. He just smiled to himself, grabbed his boxers and slip them on then he grabbed a pair of dark blue jeans and he then grabbed a shirt that was on the floor and his gold Rolex watch. He picked up his wallet and a set of keys he slipped on his black socks and his white trainers he stood up from the bed and walked up to the front door and walked pass the two gentleman he turned to the tall gentleman and said "it is all yours," he walked straight past them and headed out of the door towards the lift he walked into the lift and pressed zero on the lift controller and heading down pulled out his phone and then look as he opened up the internet on it and started tapping away on it. He wrote busses from London to Dorkchester he noticed that there was a bus leaving from London to Dorkchester in two hours. He tapped away and book a one way ticket to Dorkchester then dialled a number on his phone. The voice on the phone said "Happy taxi?" Logan asked for a taxi for as soon as possible to take him to the bus station. The voice on the phone said "We will be there in ten minutes." Logan put his phone into his pocket and looked up to the sky and waited until the taxi pulled up and Logan open up the taxi door and he jump into the back he was taken to the bus station. Logan saw the bus. He got out of the taxi, paid the driver, walked over to the bus station and stopped into the little shop and grab a bottle of Fanta and some crisps and headed to find his bus. Logan saw his bus which was number 88. He got on the bus showed the driver his phone which had the details of his ticket that he booked. He then looked down the bus and saw the bus was full of people. In the first row seat there were two very hyperactive children jumping up down on the seats and behind them there were their mum and dad. The Dad was reading the paper and wasn't paying attention to the children whilst the Mum was trying to calm the children down. Just behind them were a couple, they were kissing each other and another gentleman, who was on his phone and seemed to be shouting down on the phone to someone. Then in the last row a scary looking girl; she had purple hair and a dark black jacket. Next to her in the right side seat was a young nerdy looking guy, he looked nervous. Then in front of him there was a lady with her dog, the dog was sitting on the seat and she was fussing over him. Then in front of them was an old lady who was staring out of the window. Logan decided that this is where he would sit he thought that she looked the most normal. In front of her were two nuns and then in the final row were two young very attractive ladies holding hands. Logan walked to the seat but before he sat down he asked the lady "Is this seat taken?" She looked at him and just shook her head, he then sat next to her. The bus engine started up and it started pulling away from station. Logan heard this voice "Why so glum? What's your story?" Logan turned and realised it was the old lady and he then, "I'm heading back to my home town after twenty years to sell my uncle's house and his bar and make a new start somewhere." The lady looked at him and then replied "Look we are going to be on this bus for over five hours. I have lived eighty five years and I can tell when there is something more going on. Why don't you start from the beginning and tell me how you come to be on this bus."

Logan looked at the old lady, smiled and said "Okay I'll tell you my story."

"It started when I was eight, I was playing football for my local team when I was scouted by Chelsea, they offered me a contract to sign for their youth team and my mum and dad decided that they would sell their house and we would move to London to help my football career."

Logan looked at the lady and she was listening to every word he was saying. Logan decided that he would carry on with his life story.

Chapter 2

Youth Contract

There is a crowd of people watching a football match, it was under 8 match between Dorchester youth team vs their arch rivals Morechester. The parents were cheering on the game.

In the distance, a man stood alone, dressed in a grey suit. He was writing on a notepad. There was a young boy that was like a magician it was as if the ball was stuck to his feet, he was blessed by the footballing gods. He was whizzing in and out of the opposition players he flicked the ball over the goalkeeper and scored his second goal of the match. The final whistle went and Dorkchester players surrounded Logan and cheer him as they had beaten their arch-rivals. As the team were celebrating the man who was dressed in a suit was walking over to Logan.

He approached Logan and introduced himself.

"Hello Logan I have heard so much about you I'm the Head scout for Chelsea FC and we would like to sign you onto our youth team setup." As Logan was going to reply, his mum and dad walked over to him and asked what was going on and who the man was talking to him. He then turned to Logan's parents "Sorry Mr and Mrs Logan, I am the head scout for Chelsea FC and we would like to offer your son a youth team contract." Logan's father was delighted with this and he responded by saying "Yes yes yes we would love for Logan to join your club. Where do we sign?"

The man then looked at Mr Logan and said "I will be in contact to make arrangements for you and your family to sign the contract."

The gentleman turned and away from the family and walked to his car, a black Mercedes. Logan's mum and dad then turned to Logan and they hugged him. Logan's dad said in a very happy voice said to Logan "This is it. This is what we have been waiting for. Our dream to make it big it is finally going to happen." Logan just looked up at him and just turned and walked away without saying word.

Logan was sitting in the back of the family car. He looked back out of the window at the Town of Dorkchester. His dad told Logan "That's it son, take one last look. Now that we are moving to London, you'll never have to set foot in this shithole of a town ever again. We are going to live the life of luxury."

Logan's mum just looked at him and smiled. His mum wasn't much of a talker. Logan then just turned at looked out the window and just watched the world go by as his dad turn up the music on the radio. The Logan family pulled up to an apartment block. There was a car park entrance Logan dad was fishing in his pocket for something, he then pulled out a piece of paper and on which were four numbers written down.

He pulled up the car park where there was a keypad, he then looked at the paper and typed in the numbers, the security gate opened up and they drove into the carpark. Logan's dad then pulled up and parked up and the family got out the car. Logan's dad opened the boot where there was one large suitcase. They walked up to the door of the lift and the pressed the button for the top floor. The lift moved up to the top floor where the door opened. There was long corridor and at the end of it, the corridors there was a door with the number 201.

Logan's dad said "Here we are, this is it, our new home," He opened the door and they entered. It opened up to the living room. There was a black L shape sofa and in front of that there was a black coffee table then on the wall there was the biggest television Logan had ever seen. Logan's dad put the suitcase on the floor and in a very excited voice said, "Let's take a tour." He grabbed Logan's mum's hands and pulled her to the first room that was on left. This was the smaller of the rooms inside was a single bed with a mirrored wardrobe and on the wall a tv. He then pulled Logan's mum into the next room, this was the larger of the bedrooms inside was a king size bed with a mirrored wardrobe and off to left was an ensuite shower and toilet. Logan's dad had the biggest smile he had ever had in his life, he was like a kid in a candy store. He was overjoyed with excitement. Logan's dad then pulled his wife over to the other sign of the lounge, where there was the main bathroom. This room had a large Jacuzzi bath and toilet. Just as Logan's dad was going to pull his mum Logan grabbed hold of his mum and pulled her into him as they walk into the kitchen. The kitchen was all built in there was a silver oven and their chalk slated work top and then kitchen had silver cupboards, a slate worktop and silver oven.

Logan's dad cried out in a very happy, buzzing voice "I think we are going to enjoy living here, the rest of our stuff is arriving Thursday. We better get an early night as we have got to be up early as we have got to be at Chelsea for the morning." Logan went into his room and slammed the door behind him and collapsed onto the bed.

Logan was awoken by a loud bang he looked at his watch walked over to the door. He opened the door slightly and through the crack in the door he could see his dad he was stumbling around the kitchen. Logan knew that his dad had been out drinking. He noticed some pink lipstick on the collar of his dad's shirt. Logan closed the door and then returned to the bed until his alarm woke him in the morning. Logan got up and got himself dressed. He wore blue denim jeans with a blue T. shirt which had on wolf riding motorbike on it. Logan walked into the kitchen his mum was already making some breakfast. Why his dad was in the lounge area drinking a cup of coffee. Logan's dad turned to him and said "Good morning champ. Are you ready for the first day of the rest of life."

Logan didn't even acknowledge his dad, he just walked over to his mum and gave her a hug. She just gave him a smile and handed him a plate with a good breakfast. Logan sat at the table and enjoyed his morning breakfast. Once they had finished breakfast they went to the lift, and down to lobby. Out by the front door there was a taxi was already waiting. They jumped into the taxi and headed off. They pulled up at Stamford Bridge. Logan looked out of the window, he was speechless. This was his first visit to a sports stadium. The size of it took him by surprise they got out of the taxi there was a man who was wearing a track suit it had the Chelsea logo on it. He walked over to them and introduced himself.

"Good morning I'm Dan Striker, I am assistant to the team I will take you on a tour of the stadium and grounds and we'll finish up with some tea and cake and then we will sign your youth contract". The tour started and they were taken into the changing rooms. The pegs had some of the current player's shirts laid out their names and shirt number on them. Logan was just mesmerised by this. He was holding his mum's hand all the way round. The tour of the grounds took them from the changing rooms to the stands of the ground. Logan was just taking it all in

The man was talking about the history of the club and was talking to his dad but Logan was not listening he was just picturing the stadium full of people. He was tapped on his shoulder by his mum. The tour was carried on. Logan's dad was still talking to the man, Logan wasn't really interested on what was being said, he was just holding onto his mum hand as they made their way to the pitch. Logan's dad said to him "Just imagine sixty thousand people cheering your name as you go on to score the winning goal in the Champions League."

Logan felt another tap on his shoulder, his mum gave him the biggest smile and winked at him, his mum could say many things with a wink. With a smile the tour was concluded and they ended up a room which it looked like a boardroom of sorts. There were two piles of paper on desk, with pens on either side. There was a lady standing by the table, wearing a blue dress. She had blonde hair with a strand of blue that came across her left eye. In her left hand was a bottle of water and in her right hand she had a Chelsea shirt. Printed on the back of the shirt was "Logan" They walked over to the table. The man was talking to Logan dad. Again he wasn't really paying attention, it just seemed to be a lot of mumbo jumbo. The lady handed Logan the shirt he slipped over the top of his t shirt Logan's mum was taking lots of pictures of him. She then smiled and said, "I am so proud of you. You are my little star and I want you to know that I am so proud of you I will be here every step of the way watching you from stands and cheering you on."

She then she gave him the biggest hug she ever given him. There was a photographer who took pictures of Logan and his family as they posed with the contract and lots of him posing in his shirt and with a football. Once this was concluded they headed out of the club. Logan was holding onto his mum's hand.

Logan just turned and out of the corner of his eye he could see his dad talking to the young lady. He handed her a piece of paper, he then gave her a kiss on her cheeks before following to catch his wife and Logan up.

Suddenly the bus stopped. In shock Logan and the lady were thrown forward. The bus driver called out "Sorry ladies and gentleman there seems to have been a crash ahead, looks like we may be here for a while." The lady turned to Logan and asked him to carry on with his story.

Chapter 3

Mum No More

Logan looked at the old lady and smiled. He carried on telling her about his rise up a youth ranks. Logan told her how London life was a struggle for him and his family and his mum became ill and about her death.

Logan was awoken by a loud bang, he jumped out of his bed and ran out of his room and found his mum laying on floor. He was calling out for his dad. Logan got louder and louder shouting for his dad but no answer. There was a knock at the front door. Logan got up and opened the door there was a man and lady standing at the door. "Hello is everything okay we are your neighbours and could hear shouting,"

Logan seemed to have lost his voice. He just pointed to his mum. The man rushed over to her and he pulled out his phone and was talking on it saying we need an ambulance. Logan felt the lady grab his hands. Within what seemed like a lifetime the paramedics arrived. They were putting stickers and leads all over Logan's mum. He was very scared and one of the paramedics came over to Logan to talk to him "Hello young man I'm the lead paramedic we are going to have to take your mum to hospital for some tests, as she is very poorly."

Logan was crying. The neighbour was hugging Logan tightly and she looked at him and said "You can come and stay with us while your mum is getting better." Just then Logan's dad came stumbling into the room. With slurred voice he started to ask "What the fuck is going on here? What are you doing in my house?" The lead paramedic responded by saying "Your wife has collapsed and was unresponsive on our arrival. We have been able to bring her round and she has regained consciousness, but we need to take her to hospital for test and get her medical attention." Logan's dad then looked at the lady that was holding him and yelled "Who the bloody hell are you and what are you doing with my son?"

The man said "We are your neighbours. We heard your son screaming and we came to see if he needed any help. When he let us in we found your wife on the floor we then dialled nine nine nine." Logan's dad starting waving him arms around and he responded by saying "Well thank you but we have got this under control, you can go now."

He ushered them out the door. The lady turned to Logan as she was leaving and said to him "If there is anything you need, we are just next door, anytime just come and see us." Logan's Dad then shut the door in her face. Logan's mum was then put onto stretcher as and she was being taken out, Logan gave his mum a kiss on her hand.

It was a few days later when Logan went to see his mum in the hospital she was wired up and there were all sorts of machines beeping and making noises. Logan thought it sounded like a disco with all the beeps. Logan's dad was talking to a doctor with a raised voice. Logan's dad was getting angry at the doctor and was pointing and waving his arms around. Logan wanted to know what they were saying so he moved closer to the door, he could just make out that his dad was saying to the doctor "so your're

26

telling me that she is going to die and there nothing you and so called science can do to help her."

Logan's dad saw that he was trying to listen and screamed at him. "Go away you stupid boy, this is not for you to hear." Logan just started crying and he ran off down the corridor. Logan found a quiet area and hid down on the floor. Logan heard a soft deep voice as he look up he saw an elderly man he had a white big white beard he looked a bit like father Christmas. The man was asking Logan "Are you okay young man? you look sad, do you want to talk about it?" Logan looked up at the man wiping his eyes from where he had been crying and told the man, "My mum is dying. It isn't fair, she promised me that she would watch me play for Chelsea and cheer me on from the crowd. It just isn't fair." The man looked at Logan and responded by saying "Just because your mum is not there in person does not mean she is not there with you. Your mum has been called back to heaven by God and she will be watching down on you." Angrily Logan snapped at the man "God shmod, I need my mum why does God need her surely he has enough mums in heaven already, he doesn't need my mum. Why can't he just leave her with me?"

The old man responded by saying "God has plans for us all and he needs your mum with him but she will watch over you."

Just then Logan's dad grabbed him by the arm and shouted at him "What do you think you are doing? You can't go running around the hospital. Now come on, we are going!" he pulled him buy the arm and dragged him. Logan looked back and saw the Father Christmas gentleman waving at him.

Over the next few days whenever he wasn't training or playing matches for the Chelsea youth team, he would spend time sitting by his mum's side, holding her hand wishing she would get better. Logan's dad would spend most of his time talking to the nurses. He would disappear for hours with nurses and he would always come back looking like he'd been running.

Suddenly the beeping stopped, Logan didn't know what was happening, all he could now hear was 'urrrrr'. Suddenly the room filled up with doctors and nurses and Logan's dad. All Logan would remember were the curtains closing.

It was a few days later that Logan was dressed in a black suit. He was being driven up to a big, grand church, he walked up to the church and through the big grand doors. He went sat in a pew. Around him there were a lot of people. Logan recognised a few people but others he had never seen before.

The priest was talking but he wasn't really paying attention he was just looking the colourful windows when the priest said "GOD" Logan stood up and shouted "Tell God to give back my mum. I need her! I need her! It just isn't fair."

He then stood up and ran out of the church. He sat on a bench outside the church, as he was crying. A man came over and sat next to him, handed him a tissue and started talking to him

"Hello Howard. I'm your uncle, I haven't seen you since you were a little baby." Logan replied "I want my mum, I really miss her. It just isn't fair." Logan's uncle then told him "I know that your mum loves you very much and she will be with you forever." Logan's dad came over and grabbed him again. "Have you been twisting my son with your lies?" Before his uncle could even respond, Logan's dad was pulling him up from the bench and dragged him into the car Logan looked back at his uncle as they drove off. Logan was wondering why his dad and uncle didn't talk to each other.

Chapter 4

London Life

Over the next few years Logan would train and worked hard and was rising up the ranks of the youth setup and he was getting noticed. While Logan was focusing on his game, his dad was another story. Logan's dad didn't work, he claimed he was a football agent but his only client was his son. His dad would spend most of the day sleeping. The apartment would most days have half naked girls walking around. Logan would make these ladiess breakfast before they would leave. He never saw the same girl twice and most of the time there would be a pile of money sitting on the breakfast counter for the girls.

Logan was not embarrassed with seeing breasts and by seeing these girls in their underwear or sometimes they had towels wrapped around them. Logan was captivated by the lady's breasts, he found that no two pairs were the same, they had all different sizes and he often wanted to touch them to see what they felt like.

Logan would spend most of his evening alone eating alone playing FIFA on his Xbox. This would be his normal routine.

Logan was seventeen and was training with the youth team. The youth team manager came over and told Logan that he has been called up to the first team the for the upcoming League cup game against Bolton. He is to join the first team for the training session this afternoon. Logan was stunned with this and was lost for words. He grabbed his gear and headed to the locker room.

That afternoon Logan was in the changing room getting his gear and all around him where stars that he had seen and cheered from the crowd. He didn't know how they would react to him, They were all household names and he was a nobody. He started to feel that he didn't belong here and he did not deserve to be here, he felt like it had been a mistake. Just as he was doubting himself, the Manager came to introduce himself "Hello Logan I have been watching you for a long time, let's go and show the rest of the team what you have got." At this Logan jumped up and headed out to the training pitch with the megastars.

Logan did all the exercises and the Manger said he wanted a match between the reserve and the first team. Logan was heading over to the side of the reserve team when the manager stopped him and said "where you think you are going?" and showed him towards the first team.

The game kicked off and as soon as the ball touched his feet it felt like just like another game. He didn't see superstars he just saw a team in front of me. Logan showed his skill on the pitch he turned inside and out of the players. He was just outside the box when the ball came to his feet, he flicked the ball in the air and the volley smacked the ball into the back of the net. Before Logan knew what was happening the players came running up and congratulating him, even though it was just a training match. Everyone who saw it said it was a goal that was out of this world. After the training Logan was getting to leave when the Manager came over and told Logan, "I will see you Tuesday for the League cup match. You will be starting." Logan again was speechless, he took a leaf out of his mum's book and just gave him the biggest smile he could.

That evening Logan was so excited to tell his dad that he would be playing in the league cup match. He tried to call him on his phone but got no answer, so he waited up for him to come in.

It was about two thirty in the morning when Logan's dad came in from his evening out. Yet again, he had another girl with him, she was wearing a very short black dress that left nothing for the imagination. When Logan's dad saw that he was still up he growled at him, "What the fuck are you still doing?"

Logan was just full of excitement and with the biggest scream blurted out "I have been picked for the first team and will be playing on Tuesday in the league cup match," Logan's dad shouted back.

"What the fuck! this calls for a celebration," he went off to the cupboard and grabbed three glasses and a bottle of whisky he poured three shots, he handed one to the lady in the black dress and passed one to Logan and had one for himself "Cheers," he said as he and the lady downed the shot without thinking about it. Logan was just staring at the glass then Logan's dad came over and held the glass and moved his hand towards his mouth and forced it up to lips and he then yelled into his face, "Drink the fucking drink and become a man," Logan open up his mouth and drank the whisky down. He suddenly starting coughing and he felt like he was going to be sick Logan' dad was just laughing at him, he then turned to the lady in the black dress and ushered her towards the bedroom without saying another word. He left Logan holding the empty glass, then smacking the girl's bottom and went to his bedroom.

It was Tuesday evening, evening of the biggest match in Logan's life. He was waiting for his dad so he could give him his ticket for the game. Time was getting on and his dad was still not

31

home, so Logan left the ticket on the table in the kitchen.

Logan got into a taxi and headed to the ground as he pulled up at the entrance, he could already see the lots of fans buzzing around the ground buying their souvenirs. He headed off to go into the grounds and the security stopped him.

"Where do you think you are going young man? This is entrance is for players only?" he said to him. Logan looked at the security guard and he replied saying "I'm in the team, my name is Logan, I'm in the line-up for today's game." The guard started laughing and in response "if I had a penny for every time I have heard that one now clear off before I have you thrown out." Before Logan could respond his phone started to ring. Logan took his phone out of his pocket "Hello," he said the person on the other end of the phone. They angrily shouted down the phone "Where the fuck are you? Your're meant to be out warming up? Do you not want this chance?" Logan replied by saying "I'm at the entrance and this guy won't let me in." The guy on the other end of the phone then said "please pass the phone over to the guard." Logan pass the phone to the guard Logan could just make out there was a lot of screaming down the phone. He could just see the guard was turning red. The Guard then turned to him and just said to him, "You better go in, they are waiting for you."

Logan heading into the changing rooms. He saw all the players they were already changed and heading onto the pitch to warm up. The changing room was empty then Logan saw it just hanging up there. His shirt LOGAN 44! He walked over to it and just ran his hands over the shirt, he couldn't quite believe it was real.

Then in a in a very loud voice "Well get your bloody kit on and get out there and warmed up, lets show the ten thousand people out there what you got. I want you to wow them." With that Logan got changed as quickly as he could and headed out to the tunnel. He then paused, he could hear the noise, it was deafening. It was like nothing he has ever heard before. Logan just seemed to be frozen on the spot, he just couldn't move his feet at all. Then he suddenly felt a push on his back. It was the star striker, Logan turned to him and the striker said "Come on newbie, this is your moment," and with that Logan felt his feet move and he stepped out of the tunnel. The rush of the crowd was again deafening Logan had the daunting feeling that he was in way over his head, that he shouldn't be here Then he remembered what his mum had told him when he first started playing football. "You are like a magician when you have the ball at your feet and when you are playing the game just focus on the ball. This is your world, forget everything else, just do your magic." With that Logan seemed to forget about the noise and he headed over to the train with the rest of the team.

The first half of the match was a bit of a bore. Logan didn't have many touches of the ball and really didn't do much the game was nil nil it was during the half time team talk when the Manager came over to Logan screaming in his face "What the fuck are you doing out there? I can't believe I have wasted calling you up I don't think you are ready for this type of pressure If you don't show me something in the second half you are coming off and you will be back to the youth team to rot." Logan didn't say anything the buzzer went for the second half and Logan stood up and heading out to the pitch once more but this time he knew this was his last shot he had to block out the noise he had to make some magic.

The whistle went for the second half, Bolton had the ball and there was a tackle in the middle of the pitch and Logan picked up the loose ball. This was it, this is his moment. He looked up and

33

saw the goal and he started to run with the ball at his feet. He could see that one of the Bolton defenders was heading straight for him. The player came in with a sliding tackle, Logan seemed to, as if by magic flick the ball in the air with his left foot and just at the last moment he jumped over the player then with his right foot he brought the ball under control. He then could see that there were another two players heading towards him. while running towards the goal he nutmegged the first player with ease and just as the ball dropped down to the ground at his feet when he again had the ball under control. Logan was focused on the ball and the goal, he didn't see that the home fans were on their feet and they were singing his name the home bench where also of the feet the manager was jumping up and down.

Logan found himself just outside of the box, it was just him and the keeper. He stopped with the ball at his feet and he pulled back his left foot and let rip on the ball and it soared through the air like a thunder bolt and straight into the top corner of the net. The keeper had no chance in catching it. Then all of sudden Logan felt arms around him and he was being lifted off the ground. It was the big, strong Chelsea defender and was hoisted Logan up into the air to celebrate what they just witnessed.

The rest of match. Logan showed of some flicks and tricks; the Bolton team could not handle him and the game finished one nil.

When Logan was leaving the pitch after his teammate had praised him the manager came up to him. He put his arms around him and said "I will see you tomorrow for training with the first team don't be late."

Logan got home to his apartment and his dad was there waiting for him with another young, scantily clad woman. His dad shouted to him "Hurry up and get changed we are going out to celebrate. We are going on a night out on the town. Before Logan could respond to him his dad pushed him into his room. Logan put on a dark grey shirt with black trousers. Logan came out of his room and his dad said "Shit! What do you look like? Well we haven't got time for you to change. Lets hit the club." Logan then said "I'm only seventeen, they are not going to let me in the club and I have training in the morning for the first team." He replied. His dad responded by saying "You let me worry about that, you'll be surprised what money can buy."

Logan got to the club where his dad was talking to the bouncer. His dad then took him and his new lady round the back of the club and that is where they let them in. Logan walked through the kitchen where the glasses were being washed, he could see the mop and buckets in the corner then as they walked up the stairs and entered the entrance of the club. Logan could smell the smoke machine and saw the lights flashing and reflecting of the dance floor. The music was booming out, and the DJ was spinning his decks. Logan's dad headed to the bar to get a round of drinks. He handed a drink blue in colour to Logan. Logan had no idea what it was. "Get this down you it put hair's on chest." Logan dad said to him. Logan did not want to drink this drink he knew that he had training in the morning and he needed to go home and sleep, he couldn't risk turning up hungover. Logan took the glass and placed it on a table next to him and without saying another word he walked straight past his dad and left the club. Logan didn't see much of his dad over the next few months. His dad again spent most of his time out drinking, he often didn't even make it home Logan didn't care too much, he was focused on his training and playing for Chelsea. He didn't get call up to the first team but had been called up to the reserve and had been playing for them happily.

It was Logan's eighteenth birthday, he had been training all day. He hadn't heard from his dad all day, but when he got home to his apartment, his dad was standing there waiting for him he had a dark blue shirt with black jacket and trousers. His dad said "Come on chap, it's time to get changed, I have a surprise for you."

Chapter 5

The Agent

Logan's dad had organised a party at his club that he'd bought as this was he spent most of his time anyway, so it only seemed logical to buy it when it was up for sale. Logan entered the club, there was a few happy birthday banners hanging up from the lights. The place was full of people; Logan didn't recognise anyone there. Then he gets a pat on his back and as he turned around and saw some of his teammates from the reserves. The striker came up and said "Well Logan, we all thought you were a square and this wasn't really your scene but when your dad promised us a free bar we couldn't turn it down. Well let's get the drinks in lads and find us some good old whores."

They headed to the bar and Logan was dragged along with them. The striker got them all shots and they all downed the shots. Logan reluctantly downed his shot, he started to cough, after the shot his team mates all laughed at him and one of them shouted out "What a light weight!"

Then they turned to the barman and then they had another round of shots. Why they were having their second round of shots some young ladies came over and started flirting with the players. They then started playing drinking games, they were pouring drinks down the girl's breasts and they were putting burying their faces into the girl's breast and licking the drink off them. As they were playing these games and as they were getting more vulgar and cruder. Logan decided to slip away. He found a bench in the dark corner of the club and sat there, he just wanted to be alone. He wasn't alone for very long when a smartly dressed man came and sat next to him, he looked like a lawyer "Hello Logan allow me to introduce myself, my name is Mr Pucket I am a sport agent. I know that your dad currently looks after your contracts and negotiations but now that you are eighteen if you ever want to have someone else who maybe has the bigger deals and bigger contracts, just give me a call."

The man handed Logan his business card. Logan saw his dad was coming over with a very stunning looking woman, she looked as if she had been hand painted by an artist.

She had slender long legs and she was wearing red tights and just as the tights ended that is where the dress started. A red dress that twirled around her body as if had been sculpted to her body. This lady was like a hot girl just a pure beauty Logan had never seen anything so beautiful in his life. Logan's dad approached them.

"Evening Pucket I hope you're not trying to poach my son." he said to with a grin on his face.

Mr Pucket reply was swift "Of course I was just saying what a nice party this was and wishing him a happy birthday and my present is the one parked outside."

He then handed Logan a set of car keys and stood up from the bench and walked away; as he did so he turned to Logan and just gave him a wink before he headed off to the bar. Logan's dad angrily snatched the keys off Logan but before Logan could respond, his dad pushed the young lady and she fell onto Logan's lap. Logan's dad then said "This is Lora, I have been telling her all about you and she really wants to meet you." Logan looked into Lora's eyes which were blue in colour. Logan felt that he could get lost in thoses eyes. There was an air of silence, even with the music blaring away. It was Logan's dad who broke the silence he bellowed at Logan: "Well ask her to dance you nonce or she'll think you're not interested."

Logan just smiled and stood up as he started to stand up so did Lora. He then took Lora's hand and lead her to the dance floor.

Logan and Lora danced together, Logan had his arms around her waist as they moved around the dance floor together. Logan felt Lora take hold of his hands and she guided them down to her bottom. She then smiled at Logan and it was at that moment that Logan fell in love with Lora. He knew that he had to have this girl, she and he were meant to be. Logan leant into kiss Lora she didn't move or flinch. She was happy for Logan to kiss her and as their lips came together Logan felt as if he was floating on air. Her lips were like tasting candyfloss just so sweet he didn't want to stop kissing these lips.

He didn't even bother about breathing he just wanted more sweet candyfloss. Lora leant into Logan ear and whispered "Shall we get out of here and have little one on one fun."

Logan shouted out, "Oh yes!"

The whole club looked at him, he didn't realised that he shouted out so loud. A little embarrassed he grabbed Lora's hands and led her away. He saw his dad with a tart in the corner, he had his hands down her skirt and she had her hand down his trousers, they didn't care who could see. Logan walked up to his dad grabbed the keys from his pocket and without saying anything, he and Lora headed out of the club. Outside, the street lights lit the street and just in front of the club there was a blue Corsa Logan took the keys pressed the key, fob and the car unlocked. Logan then took Lora to the car he opened up the door for her then he got into the driver's side. They got in the car Logan started the engine and as they pulled away from the club and drove off Lora said to Logan "Why you are playing with your gear stick? I could play with another stick?"

Lora started to run his zipper down she then put her hands in his trousers and moved her hand around and said "Where is it? I think someone's hiding."

Logan stopped talking, looked at the old lady and said, "Sorry, this bit gets a little racy I could skip this part," he asked her he was shocked by the response.

"Don't be silly I may be over eighty years old but I have seen and done things that would make you squirm and I read fifty shades and I found that quite tame,"

He laughed and carried on his story. Lora was moving her hands in his trousers "Oh wait, there it is."

With a firm tight grip she pulled his penis out, Logan was in too much shock to say anything he thought she was a shy girl yet she seemed to be a totally different person now that they were alone. Lora started rubbing her hands up and down the shaft of his penis. Then she turned herself and bent down to the top of his penis and she started to tease the tip of it with her tongue, she was running it around the head of the penis. Logan was finding it so hard to concentrate on the road almost swerving the car.

Then, without warning Lora take her mouth and put her lips over top of his cock she started to move her mouth up and down his penis. Logan was just so overwhelmed with sensation.

He suddenly stopped the car Lora stopped the motions, with her mouth still around his erect penis. Logan stuttered "We are here." Lora took her mouth from his penis pushing his erect cock into his trousers and turned to Logan and said "Well lead the way big boy."

Logan took Lora's hands and they got out of the car they headed into the apartment block, they get into the lift. while in the lift Logan was looking at Lora while still with his still erect penis in his trousers. He was waiting for the lift to reach the top floor. He wanted Lora now! He felt he had found his soulmate. He pushed Lora to the wall and started kissing her, their lips locked together. Lora started to unbutton his shirt and she takes his shirt off and throws it to the ground. She then moves her hands and unbuttoned his trousers and unzipped them. Next she pushes his boxers down to his feet. He was standing in the lift with his trousers and pants down by his feet. His penis was standing at attention for Lora. Logan take his hands and unfastened her dress and it dropped to the floor, to Logan's amazement Lora had no knickers on, she was standing in front of him now with just her red bra on, he noticed that she had no hair around her vagina but he thought this was normal, he had seen a lot of breasts from the girls that his dad had round but this was the first vagina. Logan again stuttered and said "I don't know what to do now, this is my first time doing this."

Lora then pushes him to the floor and smiled at him and said "Don't worry I will take care of you." Logan was laying on floor of the lift with his erect penis. In front of him was this beautiful, naked woman. She pulled condom out of her purse and rolled it out covering his cock Logan gave a gentle laugh. Lora asked him what was funny. Logan replied by saying "I now have a blue cock."

Lora laughed as well, she gently guided his blue cock into her she says "As it's your first time it won't last long but with practice it will get longer."

Lora started to lift her bottom up and down slowly.

41

Logan could feel her vagina tightened around his penis. The pleasure that she was giving him was like she was drawing him into her. He felt so connected to her. As she started to move faster he could feel his penis getting tighter and tighter, like a volcano ready to erupt. Just as Logan felt himself ready to explode the lift door opened up and just as Logan screamed out "fuck me," an elderly couple were about to step in the lift. The man turned to his wife and said "We will wait for the next lift," she replied by shouting out "disgusting."

The lift reached Logan's floor and he and Lora grabbed their clothes from the floor and headed to his room. Logan and Lora spent the night having sex until they fell asleep together. The next morning Logan awoke to find Lora had already left the bed, he went out to kitchen. He saw his dad was talking to Lora. He was giving her money, he then kissed her on lips and slapped her on her arse. Logan's dad saw Logan and called out "Well done champ, you're now a man. I think it's safe to say she was worth every penny."

Logan screamed back "What the fuck dad! You paid someone to fuck me? How messed up are you? I thought she liked me."

Lora then said "This is too much drama for me, I don't get paid for this I'm out of here."

She then walked passed Logan, giving him a kiss on his cheek as she walks out. Logan then carried on screaming and his dad "I honestly can't believe you would do this to me."

Logan's dad replied "I was helping you've been so focused on football and you've been stressed lately and you needed sexual release." Logan angrily replied with "For Fuck's sake. I felt that Lora and I had a connection not that she had been paid to like me."

Logan's dad's response to this was "Oh my god you fuck someone for the first time and you think your're soul fucking mates."

His dad started to laugh. Logan shouted out at the top of his voice: "You know what dad, you're fired." Before Logan's dad could even reply to this Logan was already walking out the door Logan could just make out that his dad was screaming "You can't fire me." Logan pulled his phone out his pocket and the card the agent card that he was given. He called up and he asked the agent to meet up.

Logan and the agent were sitting together in the café, The agent started talking "You won't regret this, Logan sign with me and I will make you a star I have already had some offers for you, there are a couple of German teams and French teams very interested and they all want you in the first team. As your youth contract is up we should sign for one of them."

Logan responded by saying "I don't want to leave England to play football."

In response the agent said "This is what all the young talent is doing, going abroad to understand the European league this will improve your ability and make you a better player and then you can come back to England as a star trust me."

Logan quickly said "Okay I trust you and anything to get away from my dad."

Logan signed the contract and shook the agent's hand. His new agent said "Welcome to stardom. I will make you a megastar you won't regret this."

The next few days Logan would avoid his dad he then received a call from his agent telling him to get his passport as they heading to Germany, as Wolfsburg wanted to offer him a deal.

Logan and his agent met at the airport and were taken through to first class. Logan had never flown first class before, he didn't know what to expect. His agent said "From now on you only travel in style." Logan was taken to a posh hotel and in the hotel restaurant was the Wolfsburg manager and director of football. The director of football introduced himself and started to talk: "I have been watching your career very closely and believe you have natural talent and we want to make you the next success story to come out of Germany. We feel you should be in the first team and playing against the world class players."

The manger added: "Logan, looking at what you can do with the ball is like an artist painting a masterpiece - for some reason the manager is keeping you back but if you join my Wolfsburg revolution, we will build a team around you and we will win trophies together."

The agent said to them "I will discuss your terms with my client, we do have a few offers on table, but before he could finish what he was going to say, Logan interrupted and "blurted out I want to join you, where do I sign to get the deal done?" His agent didn't look happy but responded by saying; "Well, it looks like we have a deal."

They setup for Logan to have a medical the next day and this is where they will sign contract. The next day the medical was completed and contract was signed. Logan returned home to collect his belongings and he wrote a letter to his dad: Dad I have signed with Wolfsburg and am moving out. My agent has got me a house in Germany that I will be moving into I will give you call once settled to invite you round.

"Welcome! Have we got a match for you. We have Wolfsburg against Bayern Munich and Wolfsburg have their debuting wonder kid from the Chelsea youth team who has been thrown into the starting line-up. Well the Game is underway.

Bayern have a corner, it is crossed, it is headed out. Logan has picked it up just on the edge of the box he turns on the ball and he is running down the pitch, the Bayern players can't get close to him he's cutting through them like they're not even there, He has run the length of the pitch, he is at the edge of the Bayern box, he has just hit a wonder shot with his left foot, it is a screamer, the keeper has no chance of saving it. The Wolfsburg players are chasing him but Logan has run to the manager and he is giving him a hug. Just watching the replay he ran the length of the pitch and hit a wonder strike. Chelsea must be kicking themselves for letting him go for nothing.

What a match! Wolfsburg win one nil against Bayern and what a goal it was to win the game a wonder strike from Logan."

Logan was getting changed ready to go home when Thomas Hands another one of the Wolfsburg new breed of young talent. Hands called over to Logan "Yo Logan we are going to the bars tonight to celebrate the win and you need to come and join us we need to drink for that wonder goal." There weren't many of the Wolfsburg players that actually were able to speak English and Logan hadn't mixed much with the team. Since he joined he did his training and spent time at home alone in his house but he knew he couldn't turn this down.

Logan went out with his new team mates that evening, they enjoyed an evening of drinking. Logan was drinking his German beer when he saw a young Asian girl, Hands saw him looking at her he turns to him and Hands says "I bet you fifty euros that I can get her number before you."

Logan looked at him and him and laughed and then replied "Lets double it and the first to fuck her wins."

Both of them headed over to the young Asian girl. Hands started to talk to her. "Good evening let me introduce myself, I am Hands and I am world class footballer you probably heard of me."

But while Hands was talking to the young lady, Logan took the lady's hand and without saying a word he escorted the lady to the dance floor. They danced together, Logan lent in for kiss and they made out on the dance floor.

Hands didn't look impressed. After spending the evening dancing with the lady, Logan left the club with her they got a taxi back to Logan's house. Once inside his house Logan takes the young lady up to his bedroom, he stripped the lady of her top and skirt and she stands in the bedroom in black knickers and bra. The Asian lady then took off Logan's shirt and stripped him of his trousers. He then he stood in front of her in just his boxers he then lifts her up and throws her to the bed where he then unbuttons her bra and started to kiss from her toes, moving slowly up to her black nickers he could see the girl squirming more and more and wringing in the bed then he pulls of her black panties. Now her pussy was in front of him and unlike Lora, this young lady was not shaven she had a nicely trimmed bush hiding away her pussy.

Logan takes his lips and put his's mouth on her pussy, he then runs his tongue just on the edge of the clit he was teasing her. He then inserted his tongue into the pussy licking her sweet juicy pussy, in and out his tongue would go. The Asian lady was shouting out in delight until she screamed out "Please fuck me."

Logan pulled his tongue from her pussy and pulled off his shorts, he put a condom on his cock and he guided his cock into the Asian and her awaiting pussy, it was drawing his cock into her. Logan started moving up and down and slowly building up speed. Then as he was building up speed the girl was screaming "Oh my god, more more please oh shittttt!"

Logan was building up speed and hitting her pussy harder and harder he was tugging on her bare naked breasts. He then took his mouth and started to suck on her left breasts and as he was sucking on her tits and then she screamed out "Holy shit I'm cumming," and this is when finally he uttered out "oh fuck I'm cumming too," and he shoots his load into the condom. Logan rolls of her. He takes the condom of his cock and goes into the bathroom and put it the bin. He went to the toilet and washes his hands then return to his bed and finds that she had fallen asleep. Logan picke up his phone from his bedside cupboard and he takes and picture of the naked Asian in his bed, he then finds Hands in his contacts and sent the picture to Hands with a smiley emoji.

The next day at training, Hands come over to Logan and gave him one hundred euros, over the next two seasons. Hands and Logan have a friendly rivalry on and off the pitch. If Logan scored a wonder strike, Hands would score one next week and if Logan scored a hat trick Hands would then do the same. Off the pitch they would do the same, they would compete with each other, who they could pick up and take home and fuck and they would make sure they would send each other picture of their conquest. They became great friends and really enjoyed the competition. On the brink of the third season Logan and Hands were looking forward to another year of scoring on and off the pitch adding to their collection.

Logan's agents gave him a call and told him that Wolfsburg had accepted an offer a bid for him for nighty nine million euros from Real Madrid and they have arranged for a private jet to take him to Madrid for a medical and contract signing. Logan wasn't sure if he wanted to leave Wolfsburg he was really enjoying his football and had settled to life in Germany. The agent convinced Logan to trust him and the proposed contract that was being offered was huge and he would be stupid turn it down as these offers don't come around everyday. Logan told his agent to make the arrangements.

Logan met up with his agent at a private airport where they boarded a private jet. They treated to wine and drinks. Logan was sitting on the jet when he gets a message from Hands and he wrote: I have been hearing rumours that you are leaving to join real Madrid, I guess you got fed up of being in my shadow.

Logan reply to his message and wrote back: I have got bored of beating you, I am going to look for real competition. While Logan was sending the message he also noticed one of the air hostess was smiling at him.

Logan got up and said to the agent "I am just going to the shitter." as he walked past the air hostess he whispers in her ear "follow me." Logan walkked to the bathroom followed behind was the air hostess. They both go into the bathroom. Logan lifted the hostess and planted her on the sink. He ran his hands up her thighs and pulled down her knickers, he then pulled the zipper of his jeans and pulled out his already firm cock and he rammed it into the air hostess. The plane started to have a little turbulence but this just added to the excitement. As Logan rammed his cock in and out of her pussy. The air hostess was screaming out "Oh my oh my oh yes that is it."

48

Just before Logan was about to cum he knew that he didn't have a condom on and knew he had to pull out. So as he felt the urge he suddenly pulled out and the air hostess screamed "not on my uniform," and she jumped off the sink and took his cock into her mouth and Logan blew his load into her mouth. Logan had seen this in a few porn films that he had seen where they did this but he had never done this with anyone before. He enjoyed this new experience, not only had he joined the mile high club, he had shot his load into her mouth. The air hostess swallowed every drop. She pulled her mouth from his cum covered cock and licked her lips. She grabbed some tissue and wiped the cum residue from her mouth. She pulled up her knickers as Logan did up his flies, they both left the bathroom Logan return to his seat and smirked at his agent he then pulled out his phone from his pocket and looked for Hands number and sent him a message and wrote "Well guess who has just joined the Mile High club."

Logan joined Real Madrid that season, he moved from his house in Germany into a studio apartment in Madrid. Also during this summer Logan was called up for a friendly for his first cap for England at Wembley.

Logan played in the friendly, it was against Mexico. Logan didn't do much in the game and was substituted and half time. Logan while he was in London and before Logan returned to Spain he decided that he was going to see his dad. Logan went to his apartment and let himself in but his dad was not home. Logan hadn't spoken or seen his dad since he left to go to Germany.

Logan waited for about three hours until his dad came home. His dad entered saw Logan waiting for him. His dad said "Oh look at the superstar."

Logan asked his dad "How have things been dad? You look

well."

Logan's dad angrily responded "Dad, Dad. I was fired as your Dad I have no son now, piss off." Logan said "But Dad come on I fired as agent but you will always be my Dad."

Logan's Dad then responded by screaming "I have no son, you're fired as my son. Now fuck off back to your new life in Madrid I never want to see you again. I don't need you or want your help."

Logan tried to speak again but his dad just pushed him out of the door and slammed it in his face. This was the last time Logan saw his dad and three weeks after this his dad hung himself. Logan didn't know that his dad had gotten himself into debt but he also was being investigated by the police due to a rape allegation. His dad couldn't cope with it anymore and took his own life. This had big effect on Logan. On and off the pitch his game started to suffer and he really didn't settle in Madrid. What should have been a dream move started to turn into nightmare. Logan started drinking and was screwing anyone he could, his fitness levels started to drop and it started to show in his matches.

The old lady looked at Logan and said "I am so sorry for your loss you must not blame yourself for this, it wasn't your fault. How did you turn things around?"

Logan responded by saying "Well, while at Madrid my agent called me up" and Logan started to talk about his agent.

"Logan, I have a deal for you from Ajax. They would like to take you on loan. They will pay fifty per cent of your wages and maybe this will help you get back on track. They have a flat already lined up for you." Logan agreed to go on loan to the Ajax for the season. This is where Logan would meet someone who would help him get back on track and get onto the right path.

Logan had been staying in his flat for a few months and playing average football and again he was out drinking and he found the temptation of the prostitutes and spent his wages on them most evenings but one evening he met his neighbour. Logan was just coming in from an evening out of drinking and fucking. He was very drunk and fell up the stairs. He slipped and banged his head on his door. His neighbour was awoken by the noise he came out of his room and found this drunken man on the floor. He helped Logan into his flat and laid him out on his sofa. When Logan woke up in the morning he didn't know where he was. He looked around his room he could see there a statue of Jesus on the cross and in the right hand corner he could see a bible.

He then heard a voice this elderly gentleman who walked in with a pot of tea and started talking to him "Good morning it looks like you had a rough night. Here, drink this, it will help you to recover." Logan responded by saying "Where am I and what am I doing here?" the elderly gentleman responding by saying "I am your next door neighbour I found you passed out on the floor and brought you in here to help you out."

Logan angrily replied "Look mister I don't need any help from anyone I am okay on my own."

The gentleman then replied "Everyone needs help and God is there to help everyone."

Logan then responded by saying "God. Look, thanks for tea but I haven't got time for you preacher."

The gentleman then responded by saying "Logan if you don't change what you are doing you are going to waste that natural talent but if you work hard you will reach your full potential. I was like you, I thought I was untouchable and thought

51

nothing could stop me I was drinking and partying then one night I was in a car accident. This is when It happened. God saved me, he helped me and that moment my life changed for the good." Logan then responded by saying "Look mate I don't want to be rude or anything but I am a footballer what do you know about what I am going through."

Then Gentleman passed Logan a picture and it was a picture of team of players holding a cup. Logan asked "Who is this?" and the gentleman replied by saying that it was him. "I was like you, a footballer and like you I enjoyed to party and if wasn't for God I don't think I would have survived. I wasn't a big mega star like you but I won my fair share of trophies and I partied hard, fucked a lot of woman. But I wasn't happy until God came into my life and helped me. This is when I was truly happy."

Logan got up, slammed the cup on the table and walked out without saying anything else and went to his own flat.

Chapter 6

New Found faith

Logan had spent the evening after training he went to another bar, he picked another girl and took her back to his flat. Just as Logan was going to insert his penis inside her he started to think about what his neighbour had said to him. Just as his cock was on top of her pussy he stopped and rolled over and shouted out "ahhhh I can't do this anymore." He sat up, from the bed and found some shorts and slipped them on. He left he his flat and knocked on his neighbour's door, leaving the naked girl in his bed. She was gobsmacked and didn't have any idea what was going on.

As his neighbour opened his door, half asleep, not knowing what was going on, Logan screamed in his face "What have you done to me? I have a fucking hot bird in my bed and I was about to give her the fucking of her life, yet you got into my head with your "change your ways" talk I was happy with my life the way it was."

The neighbour looked at Logan and replied "Now were you really happy screwing your way through Europe?"

Logan angrily responding by saying "Happy? What's that got to do with it?"

His neighbour then responded by saying "Logan I can see that you are hurting," Logan turned and replied to him by saying "You have no idea what is going on with me. Your're just some old preacher, you know nothing about me or understand what I am going through. You're a dirty old preacher, you can't understand."

His neighbour then asked Logan "Do you really think that you're the own only person that has had shit to deal and suffer?"

Logan stood up and shouted at his neighbour "Look, I don't know who you think you are and you think you can preach to me. Look, God turned his back on me I have been on my own for years. I have not needed anyone and still don't. Just leave me fucking alone." Logan get up and heads into his own flat slamming his front door. When he get into his flat it has been trashed, his clothes were thrown all over the place, his television had the word 'prick' written on it in with pink lipstick. Logan collapsed in his bed.

The next morning Logan woke up and notice that by his front door there was a newspaper on the floor. Logan picked it up and looked at the date, it wasn't a recent paper it was from forty years ago. The headline read: HUGE CAR CRASH INVOLVING ZIMMERMAN. Logan was intrigued about this article. He sat down in his chair and starting to read this newspaper. It said that Zimmerman, a Dutch world footballer, who was on shortlist for world player of the year, was behind the wheel of his car, highly intoxicated, when he collided with a wall. The fireman had to remove Zimmerman from the car, witnesses say that it appears that Zimmerman legs were crushed. Logan was looking at the pictures of the scene there was photos of the car and what was left of it. The front of the car was smashed in, the roof had been removed. Logan threw this paper on the floor and got dressed ready for training.

After returning back from training Logan noticed that there was another paper on the floor. He then picked up this paper and read the headlines: Zimmerman Suicide Attempt Failure. Logan again started to read this article. It said that emergency responders tried to save Zimmerman's life after he was found in his room after taking a supplement of drugs. In the article it said that Zimmerman is doing well after a failed suicide attempt. There was a comment from Zimmerman's former Manager at Ajax, I am sad to hear that Zimmerman is struggling since his accident and hopefully now he is able to get the care he needs." Logan again was not interested in this article and he threw this paper on top of the other one. He had a shower and went to bed. The next morning there was another newspaper article.

Logan looked at the headline of this one and it stated: GOD SAVEd MY LIFE. In this article there was an interview with Zimmerman. He told the reporter how he had the world at his feet and one fatal mistake took away everything from him after having his legs crushed in the accident it meant he was unable to play football anymore. H hade hit rock bottom and he felt he had nothing to live for anymore, he wanted to end it all. It was when he was in hospital and his life was hanging in the balance he felt the presence of God over him, giving him a second chance. It was at this moment he devoted his life to helping those in the need.

Logan picked up the papers from the floor and stormed round to his next door he was banging on his door.

Zimmerman opened the door, "Good evening."

Logan screamed back, "Don't good evening me look I do not want your preachy help just leave me alone."

Zimmerman then turned to Logan and said "I just want you to reach your full potential I have seen what you can do on the pitch. I feel that you have the potential to be one of the world's best. It is just up to you. If you want to, you can go out and party and fuck but when the fame is gone you will be alone. Believe me, I know. I have experienced it all this." Logan screamed out "ARRRRRRR" and stormed out.

Over the next few days Logan stopped drinking and was training harder rather than spending his evening drinking and screwing. He spent his time with Zimmerman talking and watching his matches on his old television. Logan started to notice that his game was improving on the pitch, he was enjoying his football again. He was called up to play for England again. He had not played for England since his first cap and he had a better second appearance and everything was going well. Logan had a call from his agent, he hadn't had much to do with him since his loan to Ajax. The agent said that Ajax had been talking to Real Madrid and they wanted to sign him on loan for another season.

Logan then asked his agent if he could make the loan a permanent deal as he was happy and had settled in Ajax.

It took Logan's agent a few days but he came back and told him that both parties were happy for him to join on a two year loan deal, to help him with him to improve his game and that they would be watching him carefully and he will return to Madrid a better all-round player.

Logan was happy with this deal and couldn't wait to tell Zimmerman about his news. He rushed home and knocked on Zimmerman's door but there was no answer. He found out from another neighbour that he had been taken to hospital. Logan rushed over to the hospital, Logan and found where he was and when he got to the Zimmerman's bed there was a young brunette sitting holding his hand. The brunette lifted her head up and looked at Logan and said "you must be the famous Logan I have been hearing so much about."

Logan replied "hello." The brunette replied by saying "Hi

56

I'm am Zara, Zimmerman's my dad."

Logan asked, "What happened?"

Zara then said "He was out shopping and collapsed. He may have had a stroke. They are going to run some more test on him." Zimmerman started to stir and Zara looked at him "Wakey wakey, sleepy head."

Zimmerman looked around the room taking in that he was in a hospital bed and in the busy ward. He then looked at Zara and Logan and shouted out. "What is going on? Where am I?"

Zara tried to calm him down by telling him what had happened "Calm down dad, you collapsed while you were out shopping and you were brought to the hospital." Zimmerman angrily replied "I don't need to be in hospital, I am as fit as fiddle, now let me go."

Just then the doctor came round "Good evening Mr Zimmerman. It's possible that you may have had a TIA, which is a minor stroke."

Zimmerman then interrupted him and said "Look mate, I'm sure that you are a really good doctor but there isn't anything wrong with me, I am sure that you have got a lot sicker patients to look after."

Zimmerman ushered the doctor away. While the doctor was is in the corridor Logan and Zara caught up with him and Zara asked the Doctor "Is my dad going to be okay?"

The Doctor then said "Well I would like to run some more test on your father but it doesn't look like he will let us see what is going on. It is possible he may start to have more TIA. As time goes onyou and your brother are going to have to keep eye on him."

Zara angrily replied "He isn't my brother he just the next door neighbour." Zara stormed off back to her dad. Logan thanked the Doctor for his help. Zara helped her dad to collect his stuff and she and Logan helped him home.

Logan spent the first season on loan at Ajax; he had an okay season, helping his team with the Dutch League title and the Dutch Cup. He would spend all his free time helping Zara with Zimmerman. Zara who had moved back in with her Dad and she and Logan began builing a close friendship.

Just before the second season of his loan deal, Zara was getting married to her life partner Sophia. Logan was Zara's best man for the wedding. Zimmerman's health had started to decline during this time and he needed nurses daily to help with medication. He asked if Logan would give her way in his place. Logan was honoured to do this. The wedding was a great occasion.

It was whilst Zara was on her honeymoon that Zimmerman became unwell and was rushed back to hospital. It was at this time that he was told that he didn't have long and it would be a matter of days. Logan contacted Zara and Sophia cancelled their honeymoon and made arrangements to come home.

It was at this time that Logan was at his side, holding his hands, crying and praying to God for more time so that Zara could be there with him.

Zimmerman, struggling to talk just said to Logan "There is a Dutch tradition that if someone ask you…" (he coughed three times) "Something on their death bed you must honour it."

Logan looked puzzled but said, "I will do whatever you ask of me, I promise."

Zimmerman waved Logan to come closer. He then whispered in his ear, "Don't go back to your old ways when I am gone, go and win me the champion's league and become a star but also you must promise me and this is the important part, you will always help and be there for your fellow man. If you help people, they will help you back and maybe you may find love. So promise me you will do this."

Logan was going to answer him, but when he looked up he

realised he had passed away. Tears fell from his eyes, he rubbed his eyes and then Zara and Sophia came in. Logan stood up and just hugged them both.

A Few days later at the funeral during the wake at Zimmerman's flat, Zara came up to Logan and said, "You know you are the son that he wanted me to be and he was so happy to have been able watch you play and he will be watching over you as you continue to succeed on the pitch. My dad always supported me and was proud of me but he was also proud to have helped you back on to the right path. Thank you for giving him that, he will be watching out for you up there."

Logan started his second loan spell and he was having a great season, scoring wonder goals and he helped guide Ajax into a surprise Champion League Final against Bayern Munich. He managed to get Zara and Sophia tickets to the final of the game.

Logan was having a great match, in the final it was two all and then Logan was given the ball just outside of the centre circle the commentator was getting excited:

"Logan has the ball, he is running, he passes to Wagner Logan continues his run, Wagner launches the ball back to Logan. Oh my. Logan hits the ball on the volley and smashes the ball and it has gone straight down the middle of the goal. Ajax are leading three two against Bayern Munich. Is this the winning goal? Can Bayern Munich, with fifteen minutes to go, can they get another goal back. Bayern kick off, wait, a missed pass. Logan has intercepted the pass, he is running again with the ball. He has just hit another shot, thirty five yards from goal it is the back of net. Logan has just won Ajax the champion's league, with the goal of season. Logan has been the man of match and has capped it off with two goals.

The ref has just blown the final whistle Ajax have won the champion League.

The Bayern players are on their feet they have seen Logan live up to his full potential today he has shown the world what a player he is The future is uncertain, will he return to Madrid or will Ajax sign him again? But that is for another day. Logan has gone into the crowd he is hugging a woman in the crowd, must be his girlfriend."

It was a few days later Logan met up with Zara at the cemetery where her father was buried. Logan had his winner's medal which he placed the winners medal on the gravestone and hugged Zara. She then said to him, "Make sure you keep in touch Mr Superstar."
They both wiped away their tears as they left,
leaving the medal on the gravestone.

Logan returned to Madrid after his second season. He hadn't barely got settled when he had a phone call from the new manager at Madrid, who had just be hired after last manager was sacked. He said to Logan on the phone "Good evening Logan I saw what you did at Ajax and I want to build a team around you and put the bad season that you had in the past and let's make some more history together."

Chapter 7

The World Cup Final

Logan returned back to Madrid and that season he started playing for Real Madrid. He was enjoying his football, scoring great goals and having outstanding matches. He was really enjoying his football. He was called back up to the England squad and went on to pick up more caps along the way. He played well in the European championship qualifiers and he was again showing his ability on world stage. That season his Madrid team won the Spanish league and cup. They lost in the semi-finals of the champion's league. He had a good season the following season. Even better for him was his Madrid side again won both league and cup and reached the final of champion's league losing to Bayern Munich. He was shortlisted on Ballon d'Or.

He helped England into the Euros semi-finals, where they lost on penalties. Logan had an amazing season. I was the eve of the third season with Madrid. His contract was coming to an end at the end of the season and he would be a free agent and end of season. He had a call from his agent saying they needed to meet up to discuss what he wants from his new contract and where he wanted to go and how much money he wanted to get. Logan told him that he would meet up with him in the local café.

Logan was waiting for his agent he had cup of tea on the table he was staring at the cup. Then his agent came in, he was on the phone Logan could just make out what he was saying "Yeah I'm just meeting up with him now I will give you a call and let you know."

He then saw Logan: "There is my star! Logan my man, how have you been? But before all that, I have I got news for you; Shanghai Port want you and they want to make you the richest player on the planet."

Logan looked bemused. He then replied to his agent "Shanghai Port! Where the fuck is Shanghai port?" The agent replied to him by saying "It is a team that play in the China league and they want you to be their global superstar for their rebranding of their new League."

Logan shouted back, "China I don't want to go to China."

"Look Logan let's think about this for moment you can earn yourself a nice little package in China," the agent replied.

"Look no offence to the Chinese league but I want to play my football in Europe, it has never been about the money for me." Logan said to his agent. The agent started to say "Logan look, just think about it this deal will make us both a lot of money."

The agent turned and left the café and got back on his phone Logan could see the agent just out of the window talking away.

It was about three days after he saw his agent, Logan entered the Madrid changing room and he noticed his bench where he keeps his stuff it was covered with Chinese take away food. It had been thrown all over his bench, there were noodles, rice, chicken balls, and chopsticks. Logan shouted "What the shit," then Logan was thrown a newspaper and the headline read LOGAN ORDERS CHINESE TAKE OUT.

In the article the reporter said that Logan is in talks with Chinese teams in the Chinese premier league when his contract is up and the end of season. It has been reported by those close to the player that he is looking to up and move to China for a huge pay-out. Logan stormed out of changing room and got his mobile and dialled his agent. He rang him five times but there was no answer. Logan was growing more frustrated with this. Over the next few days Logan was hounded by the press all wanting to know if he was going to China. He was still not able to get hold of his agent. Logan decided to get away and as he hadn't sold his dad's flat in London and as the people that were renting out had just moved out, so he decided to go home.

Logan locked himself in the apartment and turned his mobile off and hid away from the world. The news was all a buzz with 'where was Logan'? But Logan was none the wiser as to what was being reported in the news. After about five days of isolating in the apartment, Logan had run out of food and needed to get some food so he went to the local shops. He was wearing a hoodie, jumper and glasses - the world's worst disguise. While Logan was at the till someone shouted at him "yo Logan!"

When he turned around, he saw that it was a former player that he used to play with in the Chelsea in the youth team. The player came over and patted Logan on the back and said "Yo Logan, it's me, Tarrick, we played together in the youth team together before you went and travelled Europe."

Logan replied "Look mate, I just want get my shopping and go home."

Logan bought his shopping then left the shop. Logan didn't realise that he was being followed. He was getting in the lift before he realised that he was being followed and as the lift door closed he looked up and there was the former player Tarrick standing in front of him. Logan screamed "What the fuck are you doing and why are you following me?"

Tarrick replied by saying "Look I'm not stalking you or anything but everyone is wondering where you are. You just disappeared of the face of the earth. Rumours are that you have gone into rehab or that you had gone and copied your dad and hung yourself which would have been a waste of talent."

Logan wasn't very happy with this comment and pinned Tarrick against the lift wall and screamed in his face "Just leave me alone." The door lift slides open and Logan stormed out of the lift and into his apartment.

Logan turned on his TV in his room and switched on Sky sports news. The headlines read Logan has been spotted alive and well. The panel crossed to a reporter, who was outside Real's Madrid stadium. "Logan whose contract ended three weeks ago, had disappeared, since it wask reported that he will be joining the Chinese league. Nobody has seen or heard anything from him. Even his agent had not be able to contact him neither had any of the players or coachs. There was concern that he may have sunk into depression, as his father did. But we have confirmed reports that he is alive and well and spotted in London, as yet no confirmed reports of any clubs have signed him or had any contact from him."

Logan turned on his phone and he had over a hundred missed calls and text messages and his email and Facebook messenger was all full of his messages also. He decided to call up his agent. As the agent answered "Logan thank goodness. Where have you been? Do you know what you have done to my rep since you decided to just disappear."

Logan replied to him, "YOUR REP - YOU TOLD THE PRESS THAT I WAS GOING TO CHINA."

64

Then the agent said, "Look this how it works you tell the press that your're leaving for a big deal and then other clubs will then come in and put in their bids to match. Then it works out that you get better deal or we make a big money move to China a make loads of money."

"I have told you that I'm not interested in going to China and the money doesn't bother me, I just want to play football. As far as I'm concerned like you made me do to my Dad a few years ago, you're fired."

The agent said "Let's not be too rash, I'm sure I can work out a good deal for you. I thought we were mates." Before he could continue speaking Logan pressed the button to hang up on him and then turned his phone off.

A few days later his intercom went off. Logan pressed and found it was Tarrick, who shouted down the intercom "Logan let us up, I have somebody who wants to have a chat with you."

Logan pressed to let them up. When Tarrick came up he was with the old Chelsea youth team coach they both played under. Tarrick said "Oh my, you look rough." The coach went into to his kitchen and put the kettle on, he hunted round the kitchen for the teabags and made them all a cup of tea.

Then the coach said "Look Tarrick has told me about you, and it been all over the news. Now he is worried about you. Look you don't have to sign any deals. Why don't you just come and train with the reserve and get your fitness and health back and then you can see what you want to do and where you want to go and play. Just come and enjoy the game." Logan looked at both Tarrick and the coach and nodded at them. Logan and coach continued to talk about his past and how he felt. People take advantage of him. The coach got up and hugged Logan: "Maybe it's time you took control of your own choices and go where you want to go and not let people speak for you."

The coach and Tarrick left and Logan decided that he would join up with the reserve team and get his match and health fitness level up and then see what happened.

It was three days after Tarrick and coach had been round. Training day. Logan got dressed and headed to the training ground with his boots. When Logan arrived, the reserve team were already out training, so he quickly got changed into his training gear and headed out to the rest of the team. Logan ran on to where they were warming up. The coach looked and just smiled at him. They all did their warm up and then the coach wanted to have a five a side game, so Logan was on the bibs side.

One of the reserve players who had just been promoted to reserve team, looked at Logan and said "Oh looky. What we got here? Mr Superstar come to play with the second team. Oh, how the mighty have fallen."

Then one of the other players who was on his bib side said, "Don't mind him, he thinks he's the next Messi but he's more like the next Robbie Savage, but don't tell him that."

Logan laughed. The game kicked off Logan showed that although he hadn't been training for a while, he hadn't missed a step and was like lighting on the pitch, with all the flicks and tricks. He even nutmegged the cocky youth player and this got more of a reaction that the goals that he scored in the five a side game. Logan felt happy, just the feel of the ball at his feet, no stress of money or awards, just the ball and him. Later in the changing room while he was getting changed, the coach came over and told Logan "Good job, see you tomorrow."

Logan spent the next three weeks training with the Chelsea reserve team Logan would often stay once everyone else had gone, after training practising with the ball by himself. One evening Logan hadn't noticed that it had gotten really late he decided to get changed and go home. Logan noticed that the car park was pretty much empty; there were three cars. One was the night security guard's, who was there most evenings. He was eating his microwave meal watching the security monitors. There was Logan's car and the final car was the Chelsea first team manager's car. As Logan was getting into his car, there was a tap on his window. Logan looked up and he saw the Chelsea manager standing over his car. "Good evening Logan. I have heard good things about you and have been watching you over the last few weeks. How would you like to join Chelsea again and sign a contract with us? I feel that you are what I am missing from my team."

Logan looked at the manager and smiled and his response was "yes." The two shook hands and the manager said to come to his office tomorrow and we will discuss terms. Logan signed the next day and three days after this he was going to make his second debut for Chelsea. He was going to be playing in the league game against Crystal Palace.

"Welcome to live coverage of Chelsea against Crystal Palace and Logan who has just re-signed with Chelsea is going to make his second debut at Stamford Bridge Kick off. Chelsea have the ball. It has been hit out to the left. James has the ball, he crosses it to Tarrick. Through ball to Logan, one on one with the keeper, he has just dinked the ball over his head and into the back of the net. We have been playing only for a few minutes and Chelsea with the returning Logan, already on score sheet leading one nil. Crystal Palace kick off now they have the ball. What a tackle from Tarrick he feeds the ball again to Logan and Tarrick continues his run and Logan launches the ball into Tarrick's path and what a hit from Tarrick into the back of net two nil to Chelsea Logan and Tarrick have built a great partnership, they have assisted each other and they have both scored."

The game continued with Tarrick and Logan running the game. Together they were on fire Logan won the Man of the match.

Over the next few months Logan and Tarrick were the key to getting Chelsea up the table they had progressed in all the cups and Logan form had also impressed the England manager. This was the World Cup season, it was very important to all players to impress and qualify for the team for World Cup at the end of next season. Logan had a great game for his England return. Logan was again enjoying his football and he was also avoided the off-field antics that had affected him in the past. Chelsea had a great season. Chelsea came second in the league they reached the FA cup final where they won the trophy.

The second season started similar with Logan and Tarrick both working well together, both knew this was key, as they wanted to be picked for the world cup teams. Tarrick who was in Scotland team who just managed to qualify for the world cup via the playoff and England who topped their group in qualifying. Logan, that season, helped his Chelsea team win the FA cup, the league and Chelsea also won the champions league and surprising everyone Logan won the Ballon d'Or again. Logan was picked for the world cup team.

Logan phoned Tarrick as he was setting of to Mexico Tarrick had been picked by Scotland as well. They both wished each other good luck. They were in different groups and they had worked out that if England won their group and Scotland finished second in their group, they could meet each other in the quarter finals but there was long way to go. In the England group were

Nigeria, Sweden and Paraguay, so quite a tough group. Scotland had USA, Holland and Jamaica in their group, an even tougher group, so it was very unlikely that they would make it into the quarterfinals together, but they could dream. England started quite slow in the first game against Sweden but managed to pick up wins against Nigeria and Paraguay to win their group. Scotland were not so lucky, losing all three games. They only managed one goal that Tarrick scored. Tarrick called Logan as he was leaving and said for Logan to go on and win him the world cup. England played Chile in the last 16, then in their quarterfinal won against USA. With this England reached the semi-finals where they played Brazil. They won this game on penalties Logan, with England would face Germany in the Final.

"The World Cup Final, one of the biggest rivalries in the world. England and Germany. We have had a wonderful world cup, we have had some great matches and England have surprised everyone, with Logan taking the player of the tournament, helping England to the final. Can he help England win the grandest prize of them all."

Not much happened in the game, a few missed shots from both sides but nothing of note. Then in the eighty eighth minute of the match things changed.

"He is running down the wing he is one on with the keeper we are in eighty-eight minute of the World Cup final and Logan is steaming down the wing. Oh no and Hands has just steam rolled through, Logan has just gone flying through the air and Logan is in a crumble on the floor. The medical team are surrounding Logan. Logan is showing signs of pain, he is in quite a lot of distress. The ref has shown a yellow card to Hands, the England players are surrounding him they are demanding it should be a red. There is a lot pushing and shoving between the German and England players. The management team and staff are separating the players while Logan is being strapped to stretcher, he is lot of distress as he is being carried out of the stadium. Everyone is applauding the player of the tournament."

Logan didn't remember much after this as he was given morphine to help with his pain. It was a few days later in hospital, that Logan woke up and could see that there was a winner's medal and the end of his bed. His room was full of flowers and get well cards. Logan found out that his England teammates won the game on penalties. "Oh you're awake," came a voice it was a nurse who was checking his observations.

"I will get the doctor for you," the nurse scuttled off and came back with the Doctor.

"Hello Mr Logan. My name is Dr Blanco and after your injury we had to operate to save your leg and due to this injury and surgery it will take a lot of hard work and and physio to recover and get you walking again."

Logan asked "Will I ever be able to play football again please tell me I can play again?" The doctor then told Logan "It will take a lot to build the strength for your body to heal yourself." Logan screamed out "I don't care about walking, will I be able to play professional football because if I can't do this, I will die. Please tell me that I can play again."

"Logan if you want my opinion, due to your age and the years it will take for you to recover, it very unlikely that you will ever be able to play football again. It is going to be tough and hard enough just for you to be able to walk and it will be frustrating for you." was the response from the Doctor.

Logan screamed, "Leave me alone, just leave me alone!"

Logan spent ten days in the Mexico hospital before he was able to be transferred home.

Logan struggled with the physio and the pain. He sunk into deep depression. Tarrick tried to help Logan and was often there at the physio to support him and encourage him. Logan became angry all the time and this led him to start drinking, this was not a good combination with his medication. He also went back to his old ways and was following his dad's footsteps, he was sleeping with different women and some evenings, if he could not find someone to take home, he would hire prostitutes. Tarrick tried the best as he could to get Logan to come out of this, but he just couldn't help him and one evening he had enough.

He went to Logan's apartment. Logan was laying on his living room floor with a bath towel draped over him. There were whisky and vodka bottles scattered around the room. There was women's underwear hanging off the sofa. Tarrick walked over to Logan and kicked his leg "Logan wake up, what are you doing?"

Logan opened his eyes and saw Tarrick standing over him "Why are you shouting?"

Logan pulled himself up and the towel fell to the floor Tarrick covered his eyes and shouted "Put some bloody clothes on and pull yourself together. Just look at the state of you."

Logan shouted back "What do you care, least you can still play ball, what can I do?"

Tarrick replied to him by telling him "There so much you can do, don't throw away your life like…"

Logan interrupted him "Like my dad. I know what you're going to say. That I'm going to follow what my dad did and go hang myself, well I hate to tell you this but I'm having too much fun having lots of sex and this week alone I have fucked Chinese, Indian and Turkish girls, just working my way round the full take

71

away menu this week I'm ordering Burger King."

"Logan this is serious. You are not your dad and you can do more than just fuck." Tarrick said to him.

Logan then screamed back "Why do you care? I didn't ask you to help me, just piss off and leave me alone."

"Logan your dad was a terrible role model, do not follow his path, don't throw your life away. I just want to help you I am your friend."

Logan screamed "You are not my father and I don't want your help." Logan picked up his winner's medal from the world cup and launched it at Tarrick. It just missed him. Logan screamed, "Take this piece of shit and leave me alone. I never want anything to do with football and you ever again. Just leave me to run my own life."

Tarrick didn't say anymore, he picked up the winner's medal and walked away from Logan forever, only turning to look at him one last time, wiping away tears from his eyes. The woman that was with Logan popped her head out of the bedroom and she asked him if he was coming back as she hadn't finished with him yet and Logan just turned and went into the bedroom with the lady. Then there was giggling coming from the bedroom.

Logan followed this self-destruction and was also caught drink driving and his licence was suspended. After he lost his licence, Logan would spend his time sleeping around but when he was alone, he would drink and would replay the world cup final over and over again until the day he got the phone call.

"Now I'm travelling to Dorkchester to my uncle's house. He left it and his bar to me in his will, for unknown reasons, instead of being with in a strip club somewhere." Logan turned and he looked and the lady was asleep.

The driver called out on his intercom saying "We have

arrived in Dorkchester". Logan looked out the window. The town it was a small, out of the way town. Logan thought this town reminded him of Midsummer murders, a small town with one church, one pub, one local shop yet they always seem to have a weekly murder. Logan said under his lip "Hope I don't get murdered here."

The lady said, "pardon."

"Oh nothing," was his response.

Logan got off the bus just as he was about to leave, the old lady came over to him and spoke to him one last time "Young man I heard your're story and you have been on tough run but maybe your due some good luck and there may have been an angel looking out for you and guiding you home and who knows you may find something special in this town. Don't be in a rush to sell, take in the town and see what has to offer, you may even find new love, not just for the town but the people that live there and this may be what you have been looking for."

Just as Logan turned around to reply, it was as if the lady had disappeared, he could see all the other passenger on the bus but couldn't locate her. He looked around and asked a few others, but once the last person had left and the bus set off and Logan was left standing at the bus stop on his own, looking at this small town that looked like it was still in the olden days and frozen in time and had not been told about the modern day.

Logan spent the next thirty minutes trying to find his uncle's house. He had the sat nav on his phone but kept going round in circles until there was a policeman driving past, he called out to Logan "Can I help you?"

Logan looked up at the policeman and said "I'm trying to find my uncle house but this sat nav keeps sending me round in circles."

The policeman asked him where his uncle house was and if he jumped in he would give him a lift. Logan told him the address of his uncle house and the policeman said "Oh your're Stan's nephew. I am so sorry for your loss, he was a good man. What are your plans, you going to stay around for a while?"

Logan said to the policeman "Look no offence man but I don't know who you are. I thank you for giving me a lift to the house but I'm not ready to share my personal life with you." There was silence for the next five minutes until they reached the cottage. "Here we are," called out the policeman.

Logan thanked him and as he got out of the car he saw a white thatched cottage with a picket fence. The garden was overgrown but Logan could just make out the entrance it was like the secret garden with giant bushes covering over a gate. Logan walked through the gate, up the garden path to the red front door. He pulled out the key from his pocket. As he opened up the front door it creaked.

Logan walked in the house, it had a smell of stale beer. As he walked further into the cottage he saw the kitchen to the left, he could see that there was a mountain of washing-up in the sink. He looked away and thought that he wasn't going to start in there. He carried on just in front of him was the bedroom and a double bed. He decided to carry on. The next room he came upon was the bathroom. This room was covered in spider's webs. Logan said to himself "I wouldn't want to shit in there, let alone bath in there". The final room was the living room. In this room there was an arm chair, a two-person sofa, and a cabinet with lots of junk and ornaments. It was very cluttered. Logan decided to take a seat on sofa as he was exhausted from the journey. Just in front of sofa was the television. Logan took a look around the room in more detail as he looked at the door, he saw something that he had never seen in a front room before; it was an archway made out of old beer cans, this just covered the door. Logan again said to himself "my uncle was a slob."

He then looked more around the room and he noticed there were lots of framed news article on the wall and he noticed that they were about him. There were articles and pictures of his achievements. The finals he was in and his greatest matches, it was like the walls were a shrine to his achievements. Logan started to feel hungry so he decided he would brave the kitchen to see if there was anything to eat. So he walked into the kitchen and opened the cupboards, and they were empty apart from dried up sugar puffs. He then opened the fridge and was overwhelmed by the smell of rotten milk and rotten meat. Logan was gagging from the smell, he had to get out of this house. He saw, pinned to the fridge a taxi number and he remembered that he was also the owner of a pub now and they probably did food, so he dialled the taxi and ordered the taxi to take him to closest pub. The taxi receptionist said there was only one pub in the area. He said yes that one. Logan didn't want people to recognise him, so he had his hoodie up and had dark glasses on to try and disguise him, the driver arrived after five minutes and it took five minutes until he arrived at the pub. It was a small pub village pub it was called the Dorkchester Arms. As Logan got out and paid the taxi fare, he walked to the entrance of the pub. He opened the door and took a look around. There were lots of tables and chairs scattered around the pub. There was a pool table in the far left corner and a dartboard with darts left in it. Then looking on the walls, he could see football shirts in frames. Logan realised they were all clubs that he had played for. Then a sweet voice called out "Can I help you?"

As Logan looked up there was the barmaid. She had dyed

blue hair that came down to her shoulders she was in a black top that showed her cleavage. Logan walked up to the bar and asked if they served food, he had been on long journey and was starving. The barmaid replied "The chef isn't in till later as we only serve food in the evenings but I could probably rustle you up a sandwich."

Logan smiled at her and said "Yes that would be great, thank you. Can I have a glass of lemonade with it please?"

The barmaid walked into the back, Logan took a seat in the far end of the bar, just out of sight. The barmaid returned with his sandwich and glass of lemonade. As she leant over the table Logan couldn't help but admire her breasts, they were nice and perky, Logan then decided to say to the helpful barmaid "With hooters like that you should be working in hooters."

The barmaid angrily replied, " with a mouth like that your're likely to get a slap." She then headed back to the bar. Logan then turned to his ham and cheese sandwich that she had prepared for him, she had put some crisps on the plate as well. While Logan was enjoying the sandwich the radio was playing, it was a local station and after some cheesy songs had finished, the local news came on. There was talk of raising money for the church advert for Mrs Hearn's pie's. Then it was sport news and the reporter was trying so hard not to laugh and he said "Breaking News or is it really news as Dorchester FC lost twelve nil. This brings it to two years since they last won a match, probably the worst team ever. It has been reported that with being seven nil down in the first half the manager walked out of stadium and quit in the dressing room. The club did play better in the second half, only conceding five goals. What is to happen to this club, are they going to be recorded as the worst team in history? We have tried to contact the owner to discuss what is going to happen next. No one would talk to us." The barmaid decided to change the radio station and put some upbeat music on.

It was about hour until the pub got busy, a group of lads entered the bar they seem full of life and were laughing and joking. Two of them went straight over to the pool table and another two went up to the dart board. Four of them took a table and pulled out some cards. Another group sat at another table. Then three of them went up to the bar. They ordered beers for all of them. They hadn't noticed that Logan was there until one of them, a tall guy with long blonde hair, asked the barmaid who he was. She just shrugged her shoulders and said he just wanted something to eat and a lemonade.

"Well, it would be rude not to say hello and as I am the town's biggest star, he probably a fan waiting to see me." The barmaid just laughed and carried on pouring the beers that they had ordered. Two of them walked over to Logan and pulled two seats up to his table. "Hello welcome to Dorkchester I'm Tony I am a local celebrity around here you probably heard of me I am pretty big deal."

Logan looked and the two guys that decided to join him at his table. Logan then said "Can't say I have heard of you and if you don't mind, I would like to be left alone." Then, just as the blonde guy was going to speak, the other guy that was sitting next to him, who was dressed in a smart shirt and kind of looked like the policeman who dropped him off at his house said "Wait a minute your're him, the famous Logan, your uncle talked about you so much, the great superstar Logan," The blonde guy said "Don't be silly this isn't Logan," then the second guy said "It is definitely him, my dad dropped him off at his uncle's cottage today."

He then stands up and screams out "Guys. Guys. You're

never going to believe who's here, it is Logan." They all stopped what they were doing and all came over and crowded him apart from the guy who was at the bar. He looked at the barmaid as she seemed to have gone pale like she had seen a ghost "Are you okay ydon't look too good?"

She then replied "Not really, I just told my new boss that I would slap him in the face, so I'll probably be fired." The guy at the bar laughed, "Only you could do this." The group of players were all talking and there was lot of noise they were all trying to talk to Logan.

Logan then slammed his glass on the table and shouted out "You guys are a joke. If my team had played as bad as you, I certainly wouldn't be out joking around like we won. I don't know any of you and I don't want to know you, I am here to sell my uncle's house and sort out other business and I just want to be left alone. Now if you don't mind I would like to get past."

The group moved to let him out. Logan walked up to the bar and thanked the barmaid and paid his bill. He looked at the guy who was still sitting at the bar. As Logan turned the barmaid as Logan turned called, "I am sorry for saying that I would smack you in the face, I didn't know who you were." Logan said to her, "It is okay, I was rude to you and was out of line. Thank you for the sandwich and the lemonade." Logan nodded to the guy sitting at the bar and walked out of the pub and he ordered himself a taxi to take him to his uncle's cottage.

The next morning Logan was awoken by a knock at the door, he pulled himself up from the top of the bed. He decided not to sleep in the bed, he just slept on top. When he opened the door, it was the gentleman that was sitting at the bar. He was standing at the door holding a box of biscuits. He gave Logan the box of the biscuits and then introduced himself:

"Good morning. I didn't introduce myself last night. I am Harvey Smith. I would like to welcome you to Dorchester. Let me be your tour guide of the town. I was born here and work at the biscuit factory that my dad owns and I am the goalie for Dorchester FC, so ask me anything about the town, let me be your Google."

"Look buddy, I don't mean to offend you, but I don't want or need your help. I just want to sort out my shit and go back to London and never look back at this shithole again," was Logan's reply.

But Harvey was not put off by this and then said "Look you don't want friends, I get that but how about some clothes, it looked like you slept in what you are wearing. Let me take you to the clothes store and then I can introduce you to the estate agents, so you can sell the cottage if you want, but I just want to help."

Logan snapped back "Fine, I will let you help me get to the clothes shop and help me with the other shit but that doesn't mean that I like you or anything."

Logan followed Harvey to his car after locking the cottage, they drove down the street to the main strip, where there were ten shops either side of the street. Harvey parked up just in front of the third shop on the right side of the street.

It was a little clothes shop, they went into the shop and Harvey found the owner of the store.

"Logan this is Tom Elliot, he is the owner of this wonderful store and he is the centre back for Dorkchester FC."

He was a smartly dressed man, in a smart black shirt with black trousers and black leather shoes. He then spoke to Logan "Welcome Logan take a look around and let's see if we can find anything for you, the changing is just out the back."

Logan took a look around the store and picked up a few items of casual wear, blue denim jeans and some polo shirts in different colours. He went to the back of the store to the changing room. As he looked back, he could see that Harvey and Tom were talking. It looked as if they were arguing about something but he couldn't make it out. He went into the changing room. and tried on the jeans and shirts. He was happy with the fit, so went up to the till. Logan pulled out his wallet but then remembered he had no money, he had blown all his money on booze and hookers. Logan put his wallet away and then was about to turn and leave without the clothes. When Tom called out "Where are you going? You haven't taken your gear?"

Logan then hastily replied "I have left my money at home so will have to come back another day."

Then Tom said "Nonsense. I can set you up a credit account and can pay when you have got the money."

Logan turned back around as Tom placed his shopping into a bag. "Thank you and I will pay you back," Logan said to Tom said in reply to this "That is okay Mr Superstar, I'm sure that you are good for it."

Logan and Harvey left the store and thanked Tom again before they left. They headed up to the last store that was on the right side of the strip. This was the Estate agents. The store front had the name Brooks estate agents over the door.

They entered the estate agents where there were two gentleman. There was elderly gentleman and a middle aged man was next to him. They were dressed in black shoes, black trousers, white shirts and black jackets over their white shirts, both men dressed the same. The younger gentleman was one of the men that were in the pub the previous night with Tony,

"Good afternoon gentleman welcome to Brooks, how can we help you?" Tom said "Come on Gus, no need to be so formal. It's me! I'm just bringing Logan round as he is looking to sell his uncle's cottage."

He then turned to Logan, "Logan this is Augustus Brooks better known as Gus, he is a midfielder for Dorchester FC."

Logan shook his hand and then said to Gus "Yes, I'm looking to sell my uncle's house and his pub and get the best deal possible and I'm looking for a quick sale."

Gus then said "Yes, I will come round in the week to take some pictures and measurements of the cottage and the pub and we can get it on the Market and see what interest there is and what we can get for it and will be in contact with you when we have any offers. The pub may have a bit of interest, the cottage will be harder to sell but I will work my magic." Logan laughed at his magic comment and was happy for him to come and take some pictures. Gus said, "We have just got to sign some paperwork if you come over to the desk we will get them signed up."

They walked over to the older guy, as they approached Gus called out: "Yoyo Dad, this Logan, he is Stan's superstar nephew and is looking to sell the Pub and his cottage."

The elderly gentleman then slapped Gus round the head and said "I apologise for my son, he still hasn't understood what being a professional is about and sometimes needs reminding. As the owner of Brooks estate agents, it would be a pleasure to sell your uncle's place. Your uncle was a good man, a pillar of the community. I'm sorry for your loss."

Logan then said "Thank you I didn't know my uncle that well, I had not seen him in over twenty years, so can't quite understand why he would leave me these properties, so really

81

want to see this property sold as quickly as possible so I can return home and get back to my own life."

They signed some paperwork, shook hands and then left his store.

Tony then turned to Logan and said "I don't know about you but I am starving. Shall we grab something to eat, the café Spice is open across the street."

Logan was still standing and didn't move. Tony called from the other side of the road "You coming then."

Logan started to cross the road when a red sports convertible car was speeding down just missing clipping Logan. The car pulled over and the driver screamed "Fucking look where you are going dumbass."

The driver was Tony and when he realised it was Logan he said "Oh sorry Mr Superstar didn't see you there. You want to ditch this loser town and come for a drive with me. We can grab some drinks and girls. What do you say?"

Without saying anything Logan crossed the road and joined Harvey outside of the café.

Harvey looked at Logan and said, "Well, let's go eat."

They entered the café, it was quite busy. there was lots of people in the café. The waitress came over, she was in a black dress with a red apron over the top, She approached and kissed Harvey on the cheeks. "Table for two gentleman?" she asked. Harvey then said, "Logan this is my fiancé Sophie Rodgers, her dad is the policeman that dropped you off at your uncle's cottage the other day and her brother plays left midfield for Dorchester FC, he is the one is the guys that blabbed to the pub about you."

Logan took Sophie's hand and gave it a kiss and then said, "It is a pleasure to meet you Sophie and might I say you are far too beautiful to be working in a place like this you should be on catwalk in Milan."

Sophie blushed as she pulled her hand away, Harvey tapped Logan on the shoulder and said, "Logan, I hope you are not hitting on my girl." Logan just laughed as they were led to the only free table in the café.

The café was old in design with wooden beams on the ceiling. The table and chairs were wooden. The walls had pictures of the town from different ages and you could see the kitchen and the chef that was working away in there. There was an award on the wooden counter, it said "Chef of the Year" with Luke Wise's name on it. There was one waitress escorting Logan then there was another waitress on the other side of the café.

She was also dressed in the same black dress with red apron. She was talking to a family and taking their orders.

Sophie handed them the menu and asked what they would like to drink. Harvey said that they would have two beers. While they were looking over the menu, the chef came over to them. He patted Harvey on the back before moving around to Logan and shaking his hand. He then spoke to them, "Don't worry about what's on the menu guys, I will make you something amazing." Harvey then said, "Logan, I would like you to meet probably the best chef not only in the country, but the whole damn universe." Luke interrupted and said, " Let's not go over the top there." Tony carried on saying, "Okay, okay, as well as being a great chef, he also plays left back for Dorchester FC."

Luke went back to his kitchen to make their meal. Logan looked around the café and everyone all seemed happy and enjoying each other's company. The family that were eating together, the couples that were on dates - Logan felt sad, as in his life he never went out for meals with his family, even when his mum was alive. Although he had slept and been with many women he couldn't actually remember going on a date with any of them. Under his breath he said "Holy shit, I am my Dad." Harvey then asked, "Did you say something Logan?" Logan replied with "Oh nothing."

It had just occurred to him that he was just like his dad just fucking anything he can.

Luke came over with their meals, the aroma of the food was so divine that you could already taste it. Luke put it in front of them and said, "Enjoy, if you don't like this, then you have no taste."

The meal was roasted chicken with a whisky sauce with smoked vegetables with potatoes dauphinois. Luke then said, "While you enjoy this, I'm going to make you an extra special pudding that is even better than this."

They starting eating and Luke headed back into the kitchen. When they had finished eating, there was nothing left on the plates, they had both eaten everything. Luke came, back this time with the pudding. It was a Chocolate Baked Alaska with Vanilla glaze. He placed them in front of them and again "Said enjoy" this. This time he didn't return to the kitchen, he pulled up a chair and joined them at their table. They finished their meal and they both thanked Luke for this meal. Logan looked at Luke and said, "Hey if you were half as good a footballer as you are a chef, you'd be playing in the big league. That was probably the best meal I have ever had and I been to some of the swankiest restaurants around. Why are you wasting your talents in the café when you could be cooking in five star restaurants?"

"Thank you very much for that compliment. I once worked for a big chain, but when you work in a top restaurant in London things are so stuffy and stiff and you had to cook a certain way. Me, I have my own style and being here I can express myself in my food."

Suddenly there a lot of commotion and when they looked up at the entrance, they saw it was Tony and Rover, the policeman's son. They had two girls with them, both dressed in miniskirts that were barely covering their arse. One was red and the other was blue the girl in the red skirt had a pink vest top but her middle of her stomach was exposed and the girl in the blue skirt had a yellow spotted top that was very see through, that showed a black bra underneath. Tony was asking for his usual table. Then Luke said "He does one photo shoot for a calendar and he thinks he is Tom Cruise, what a joke." Logan and Tony thanked Luke for the meal Luke told them not to worry about the bill, it is his treat. As Logan and Harvey were leaving the café. Tony called out to him, "Oh look it is Mr Big Shot hanging out with Mr Loser what is this loser relief." He laughed.

As Logan had learnt from I think his mum the art of saying so much without uttering a word. He looked at the two girls that they had come in with and without any warning, he kissed the girl in the red skirt on her pink lips and then he moved onto the girl in the blue dress, and again, without any warning, he lent in to kiss her on the lips. This time it wasn't just a peck on the lips like the first one. She opened up her lips as he put his lips on hers. The whole café watched as these two complete strangers were snogging. It seemed to go on forever before Logan pulled away and gave both girls a wink before leaving the café. In the background, as they left the café, Tony and Rover argued with the two girls, who are both blushing and with big smiles on their faces.

Harvey turns to Logan and says, "Well today has been an eventful day. I'm exhausted and got training tomorrow, let's get you home."

Logan, "It's okay, I am going to have a beer in the pub

tonight before heading home. Thank you for today."

Harvey said back, "That's okay and I will see you same time tomorrow. We have only begun to touch the service of the team, I mean, town." Logan quickly replied, "What?"

But before he could say anymore Harvey was already half way down the road. Logan headed off to the pub.

Logan entered the pub, it was another quiet evening. There was one man sitting in the far corner of the pub, staring at his beer. There was a couple that were having a meal together. Then there was the same barmaid from the other night with her blue hair, this time she was wearing a red tank top and again she was showing off her cleavage. Logan walked and sat on the bar stool at the bar. Logan asked her for a beer. The barmaid brought over the beer she then spoke to Logan, "Look I am so sorry for threaten to smack you in the face I kind of have jerk reflex and my mouth speaks before my brain has a chance to catch up I don't normally threaten my boss". Logan replied, "Look sorry, I don't know your name?"

She said her name was Lucy, Logan carried on talking "Okay Lucy, I will be straight with you, Yes my uncle may have left me this bar, but I have no intention to keep it, I intend to sell, it so as far as I am concerned I am not your boss, so just treat me as you would any other customer."

Lucy then carried on the conversation by saying, "I like your honesty and I just want to know if you can do me one favour? When you sell to whoever the new owners are, if you can put in a good word for me, this job is the only thing I have, not many places hire ex-cons."

Logan looked shocked at this, and seem surprised by this to him, she didn't look like a criminal. He was intrigued so decided to pry into this more. "So, what's your story, you don't look like a big shot criminal."

She then looked into his eyes and said, "It is a long story."

Logan said, "Well, I've got all night, I haven't got anywhere to go,"

Lucy carried on, telling him about her younger days. "When I was younger, in my rebellious years, I got in with the wrong crowd, smoking shit and doing all sorts of illegal stuff but to fund our habit we started robbing a few shops here and there. We started to enjoy the rush of robbing. We then started to look at more bigger targets for more excitement, to fulfil the rush and we started to hit a few small banks. We had a knack for robbing and word got out and we were approached to hit a bigger target, a national reserve. This job seemed too big for a small group, there was just four in my gang, Toad, Ferret, me and Cleopatra."

Logan interrupted and asked her "So what was your nickname then." Lucy looked embarrassed at this comment. She stopped talking to him as she had to serve the couple a glass of red wine and a bitter. She then stayed at the other end of the bar. Logan moved down to the other end of the pub and sat on the bar stool in front of her. He then spoke to her "So, what was your nickname in the gang and you haven't finished telling me what happened?"

She carried on talking to him "Well if you really want to know, they called me Legs," Logan couldn't help himself and let out a chuckle. "So why did they call you Legs?"

Lucy then lifted her right leg and rested it on the bar.She had long, slim legs that seemed to go on forever. It reminded him of what you would imagine a ballerina's legs would look like. In response to this Logan let out a gulp "Well that is one fine leg you got there," he again chuckled to himself. Lucy seemed embarrassed but never the less, she carried on telling him about what had happened. "So where were we? Yes, there was the four of us, but the score was too big for us and to help. We get this job done we had to draft in two new guys to help us we had Gunner, you could tell he was ex-military, totally badass and then there

87

was Hatchet. Now this guy scared the shit out of me. Gunner was straight edge while as Hatchet was a god damn psycho, This is the kind of guy who, if you crossed him, would skin you,not only skin you but he would find anyone you cared about and skin them too. Well anyway, so everything about the job just didn't seem good, it just felt off and no matter what I said to the others, they just said this would be the last time."

She continued "We managed to get into the reserve without a hitch and everything was going well, until Hatchet and Gunner started to argue and in the time they were arguing, one of the guards managed to trigger the alarm. This is when all hell broke loose. Gunner shoots the guard and while he is shooting the guard, Hatchet then shot Gunner in the back. In all the commotion, me and the group get separated, with alarms were going off and people running for their lives. Hatchet was just shooting at anyone he could. He barricaded himself in and was screaming 'I will take all of you mother fuckers out before I ever go back to prison',

"I was caught escaping as the police had been alerted to what was going on and had swarmed the building. Hatchet was shot and killed by the Police and all four of us were caught. The police pressed me to flip on me, well what I thought was my friends, but little did I know they had decided that I was going to be the fall guy and they said it was me, that I had organised it and I was the brains. They all got reduced sentences and didn't spend any time in prison, but as I was the kingpin of the operation, I got five years. After I got out of prison I drifted for a while, trying to find work but due to my record no one would hire the super criminal Legs, until one day I ended up, I don't quite remember how, I was probably pissed, in this town and this pub and your uncle saw me and took pity on me and offered me a job."

Lucy looked up and realise that the pub was empty and it had gone closing time. Lucy apologised for keeping Logan so late but Logan was not bothered and thanked her for telling him about her life, she had quite an eventful time. Logan looked into her blue eyes and said "Well, it is getting late, suppose I better go and get some sleep. I think Harvey says he has more to show me tomorrow. Now, Miss Lucy, would you like me to escort you home?" Lucy couldn't help but laugh at being called Miss Lucy she replied to him with "Why what a kind offer. If I didn't know better I would think you were a gentleman. Thank you for the offer but I am already home I live upstairs, but thanks anyway, unless you need escorted home Mr Logan sir." He chuckled at this. "Well don't be spreading it around, I don't want be people to know I care. Well in that case my lady I bid you adieu."

Logan gave Lucy a smile and she smiled back at him Logan left the pub. As Lucy was locking the door, he kissed Lucy on her right hand and once again said goodnight.

Neither Logan nor Lucy noticed the dark figure that was in the alleyway. It was Roger! Hewas watching Lucy and Logan as they seemed to be flirting with each other. He pulled out his phone and called Tony He told him what he had seen. Itlooked like Mr superstar has taken a liking to his ex-fiancé. Tony was screaming down the phone, Who does this guy think he is, coming into my town and taking over, Then all that can be heard was ascream. Then a crack and the phone went dead.

Chapter 8

The Team

The next morning Logan was awoken with cupboards being opened and shut. He thought there was somebody in the cottage. He looked around the room for something he could use to protect himself from whoever was there. The only thing he saw was a rusty golf club that was in the corner of the room. He picked it up and snuck out of the room into the kitchen. He held the golf club over his head ready to swing it at whoever was going through the cupboards. Just as he was about to connect he realised it was Harvey: "Harvey what the fuck are you doing breaking in, I almost hit you."

Harvey then lifted his head from the cupboard "Logan good morning. I have noticed that your cupboards are bare, it looks like you need a trip to the supermarket."

"Harvey stop. You can't just let yourself into my place, I mean my uncle's house." Harvey was not listening and carried on looking in the kitchen cupboards and fridge,He said to Logan that he didn't have any basics in the kitchen and while he is waiting for the house to sell heneededto have stuff in the kitchen. Logan realised that he wasn't going to get rid of him, so he went back to the bedroom and got himself dressed. They then got into Harvey's car and they drove to the supermarket just on the edge of the town. It bordered between the next town over, Foxford, this town was also Dorkchester biggest rivals and the towns had spent years competing against each other.

They get to the supermarket and they grabbed their trolley and Harvey led Logan around the store and filled up the trolley. The store was busy, lots of people doing their shopping. Harvey was telling Logan about the history of the store, but Logan wasn't really paying attention. Every now and again he said to Harvey 'Yes, that is very interesting". Once they had a full trolley they headed to the tills, they were all busy. Then Harvey pushed the trolley down to the sixth till and said "this is one." At the till was elderly couple in front of them who were getting their monthly shopping. The guy at the till appeared to be of Greek descent, he had blonde hair with there was a strand of pink highlights Logan noticed. Harvey and Logan started to load shopping onto the till as the couple finished and paid. Then Harvey was high fiving the guy at the till, he turned to Logan and said, "Logan, this is Mateo. He is the coolest man in the whole of Dorchester, This man radiates style and panache, whatever that is. He also is the playmaker in the midfielder for Dorkchester FC, not only style on the pitch but also off it."

While Harvey paid for Logan's shopping, Mateo spoke to Logan, "Hey what's up?"

Logan replied, by asking him, "Where are you from?" Mateo replied, "My family are from Greece, but after my dad lost his job as a teacher back home in Greece he was struggling to get another gig, then he was offered a job teaching in England at the school in Dorkchester so we moved to England."

Harvey finished paying the shopping and told Mateo he would see him at training tonight. Logan said it was nice to meet him and he would see him around. Harvey had already loaded his car with the shopping. Logan stopped Harvey before he got into the car and said to Harvey "Look I don't know what your game is paying for all this shit, I'm not some helpless case and need saving. I may be, at the moment due to some financial errors, without funds but once I have sold the pub and cottage, I will have money again and will pay you back every penny."

Harvey was taken aback by this but in response he said "Logan, Logan, there is no secret agenda. I am just being friendly. I know that you're used to the big cities and the custom of people being helpful is strange to you. I'm sure that in the big city everyone is out for themselves but in our small town we look out for everyone, even you, this is just the way we are, I assure you."

Logan quickly replied by saying, "I guess I can be thankful for your help. I don't think I would be able to do all this on my own, so thank you." They got back into the car Harvey told Logan that he had to pop into the office on the way back to town. His dad's biscuit factory was on the way back into town.

As they drove up to the entrance of the biscuit factory he could see, just to the right in the far distance, is what appeared to be a small stadium. Logan asked "What that is over there?" Harvey told Logan "That is the Dorkchester stadium, it has been a part of the factory for as long as the factory has been a part of community. It was built to help relieve stress for the workers, then became the town ground where the club was formed." They drove up to the front entrance of the big, grand factory. They opened the main door, there was middle aged lady siting behind the reception desk. She said 'good afternoon, to Harvey and Logan as Harvey signed Logan in he was given a visitor's badge. Harvey typed in the code on the keypad on the door and it opened to allow them to walk in. As they entered the factory floor they heard the noise of the all the machines working hard and Logan could see that the whole factory floor was watching him. Harvey then saw two guys and he went over to them and said, "Logan, come and meet Cesar and Raul, they both play for Dorchester FC, they are squad players, with Raul being my understudy. I do apologise, their English is not very good."

Raul said to Logan, "Hello you work biscuits?" Logan laughed "No, no, I'm not here for a job:" Then Cesar came up with some sample of biscuits saying "You taste, good biscuits, you taste." He then handed the sample to Logan. He tried them, and the taste of these biscuit, they were ginger nut biscuits. Logan responded by saying, "These are nice biscuits."

Logan heard Harvey call out "Come on Logan, the office is this way." Logan caught up with Harvey as he stood outside his office. He was standing next a tall, well-built guy, you could tell that he had been going to gym on regular basis. Harvey called to Logan "This brick shithouse is Charles Champman or as we like to call him The Tank. He is the centre back for Dorchester FC."

Charles shook Logan's hand, he looked at the size of his hands, they were huge. He had a vice like grip when they shook hands. Logan then said "Oh my, you're a big fella. You look like you should be on the world's strongest man not working at a biscuit factory."

Charles let out a roar of laughter, "Ha ha ha ha Well I will let you in on a little secret, biscuits and football aren't where my real passion is. I dream of being a big, professional wrestler. I want to reach the big time in America."

Logan replied by saying, "You want to run around in spandex and slam men around, sounds fun,"

"Ha ha ha ha Your're a funny one Logan, not all wrestlers wear spandex but, yes, I want to slam other men to the ground." While Logan was chatting with Charles he hadn't noticed that Harvey had disappeared into the office and when he came back he patted Charles on the back, and said, "I will see you tonight for training." Logan and Harvey said goodbye to Charles and they left the factory saying bye to the receptionist on the desk. On the way back to the town Harvey said to Logan, "I have training tonight. You can come along and check us out, if you want." Logan said, "Not tonight, I'm going to have a beer, then go to my uncle's dirt hole."

Harvey dropped Logan off outside the pub. Logan went into the pub, it was busier than the night before. There was a group of ladies around the dartboard drinking and laughing away. Then he noticed the sign that said Ladies Darts Match. Logan looked but he couldn't see Lucy there was guy at the bar. Logan walked up to the bar and he nodded to the barman, then Logan asked, "Where's Lucy tonight?"

The barman replied, "This is her day off, she will be in tomorrow, what can I get you to drink?"

Logan decided not to stick around, so told the barman that he didn't want anything tonight. He left the bar and headed to the cottage.

The next morning Logan was again awoken up by the crashing noises coming from the kitchen. Logan didn't panic this time around but he did decide that he was going to freak Harvey out this time. So he got up from the bed, removed the boxers that he had on for bed. Then walked into the kitchen, completely naked. As he walked into the kitchen he suddenly heard screaming, before he realised that it was not Harvey, but an Asian lady with a mop and bucket. She started to hit Logan with the mop screaming at him. Logan retreated to bedroom. Then Harvey came into the bedroom and said, "Oh I see you have met Mia Yim. She is your new cleaner but I just want to say, in future, it might be a good idea to wear clothes when she is around."

Harvey let out a chuckle. Logan got himself dressed. He

came out and apologise to Mia for scaring her "I'm so sorry I didn't know you was here in my kitchen. Harvey didn't tell me about you, I promise it won't happen again." Mia didn't say anything, she just carried on cleaning. Harvey then told Logan that he needed to pick up meat from the butcher and also had to go to the bakers today. But just as they were going to leave, there was screaming from Mia again. This time, one of the taps in the kitchen was spraying water everywhere. Harvey managed to get under the sink and turn the water off. He then pulled out his phone, went to the living room while he is talking. He then came back and told Logan a plumber was coming round later to sort it out. Logan and Harvey left to go out to the bakers and butchers.

Logan and Harvey again go to the strip of shops. Harvey took Logan to two shops, they both had Penfold on them one was Penfold Butchers and the other was Penfold Bakers. Two guys came out of the store and approached Harvey and Logan. Harvey introduced them as the Penfold twins, Tim Penfold was the baker and Calvin Penfold was the butcher. Harvey told Logan that Tim played right back and Calvin was the right midfielder and they both played for Dorkchester FC. Their family had been a part of the town for as long as it has been founded. Tim took over the Bakers from his dad and Calvin took over from his uncle, who had no children of his own. Harvey took Logan into the Butchers first. On the deli counter there were fresh cuts of pork, beef and there was black pudding sausages. It also had fresh eggs. Calvin told Logan that all the meat and eggs were from a local farm. Harvey got his meat order then paid and they went next door to the bakers. There were fresh cream cakes, ice buns and lots of different decorated cupcakes. Tim handed Logan a cupcake that he had made, a chocolate cupcake with the centre filled with strawberry sorbet. Harvey was collectedhis cake order from Tim.

Logan and Harvey said bye and Harvey on the way out said to Tim, "See you at training tonight."

"Last training session before the League Home match on Saturday." Tim said, "Catch you later."

Harvey told Logan that he'd remembered that he needed to pop over to the private school, he had to drop some stuff off. He said that once he has done this, he could run him home, if he didn't mind Logan said that was okay.

Logan and Harvey drove up to the private school and as they got to the school, Logan thought that it looked like a castle, more than a school. It had what looked like castle turrets and at the front it had a massive gate. The building had a creepy vibe to it. They pulled up to the main car park. There was a grand door as the entrance. They entered the school and they went through the main hall. Just on the other side of this was the headmaster's office. On the door was written, "Mr Glass Head Teacher." Harvey knocked on the door of the office and a voice said "enter" from the other side. Harvey opened the door and sat behind the grand desk was the head teacher and at the other side of the desk was a young student. Harvey then said to Logan "May I introduce you to Mr Glass, the head teacher of this school and this young fine lad is Terry or as we like to call him, the mascot. As we don't have youth team at Dorchester and being only fourteen he is a part of the squad and Mr Glass also plays midfield for Dorchester FC."

Mr Glass stood up and held his hands out to shake Logan's hands. Mr Glass then spoke, "Hello, it's nice to meet you, we didn't get to talk the other night. I'm Mr Glass I am the head of this school." Then Terry said, "Yes he is the coolest head this school has ever had." Mr Glass looks at Terry "Now don't think buttering me up is going to get you out trouble mister."

Harvey then asked, "Terry, what have you be up to now?" Terry lookedup sheepishly: "Well I set off a stink bomb in the girls, changing rooms nothing major."

Mr Glass then said "I wouldn't say it wasn't nothing young man."

Harvey then said to Logan, "Terry is the town's prankster." Mr Glass told Logan the reason Terry came to this School. "Yes, Terry is a bit of a prankster and one of the reason he is at my schools and the reasons why no other school will take him is pranks: There was one prank where he also blew up his old school, he built a homemade bomb and the explosion was bigger than he thought." Terry then said, "Yes, but sir, it did make one hell of bang,"

Mr Glass did not look impressed with his comments "That is not the point. Some times I wonder if I hadn't taken and wrong turn when going for a job interview and I ended up at the wrong school, how would have my life ended up."

Logan said, "Pardon." Mr Glass then says, "Yes, it is a funny story. A few years ago I had quit my last teaching job and I had applied for a different school and on my way to the school that I was meant to go to my sat nav stopped working and I got lost and I ended up at this school. Yet for some reason it was like I was meant to find this school as the head teacher was retiring and when he saw me and we spoke he offered me the head teacher job and that was that. Now I teach and play for Dorchester FC." When Mr Glass finished talking Harvey handed him some papers and thanked him Harvey and Logan then said bye. Harvey said, "See you tonight for training." Then Looked at Terry and told him to keep out of trouble.

On the way back to town Logan asked Harvey to pull over and then told him. "Look I know what you are doing, introducing

97

me to all your teammates for your Club. Now I don't quite know what your purpose is but if I make you deal and watch your next match, will you leave me alone. My plan is to sell my uncle's house and pub, I don't want to make friends. Unlike you, I don't plan on staying around."

Harvey just shrugged his shoulders and said "I don't know what you mean, I am just introducing you to the town but if you insist on coming to watch the match I will have a ticket for you."

Harvey dropped Logan off at the pub. Logan went into the pub, he looked around. The pub was quiet again, the only person was the man sitting with a beer in front of him. Logan saw that Lucy was working tonight. He waved as he walked over to her and sat at on the. He then spoke to Lucy, "I missed you last night."

She replied by saying that it was her day off, she liked to have one day off a week, just for her, as the rest of the time she was in the pub. Logan then said to her, "What's with the guy over there he just seems to stare at the drink but never drinks."

Lucy told Logan, "He's Brett, a former soldier who, after he left the army, he struggled to fit in with normal life and became depressed. This led to drinking too much after his wife and children left him. After of all night bender, he ended up in this pub and since that day he hasn't had another drink. He started to try and sort out his life. He plays in midfield for Dorchester FC and this has helped him, but he come in every evening he's not training - orders a beer but never drinks it."

Logan said, "Wow, if I didn't know better, I would say that there was something strange about this town."

Lucy chuckled and said, "There is something special about this town."

Logan then asked Lucy what she was doing tomorrow as he

is going to the match tomorrow. "I will be working, waiting for the team to come back. They always come here for drinks after." Logan then says now he has met the whole of Dorchester FC team pretty much he might as well see them in action. Logan stayed in the pub till closing again before saying goodnight to Lucy.

Logan was again woken up to banging coming from the kitchen, this time he made sure that he was dressed before going into the kitchen didn't want to scare the cleaner. As he entered the kitchen the cleaner was there but there was also a man with his head in his sink.

Logan called out, "Hello, can I help you?" the guy pulled himself from the sink, "Oh hello Logan, Harvey called me yesterday saying you had a leak I couldn't make it yesterday, I had another job but I thought I would come first thing this morning before the match this afternoon."

He then got back under the sink and carried on doing what he was doing. When the plumber had finished up he spoke to Logan, "All fixed."

Logan said "Thank you, sorry I didn't catch your name," the plumber then replied with, "My name is David Mcfadden I am the local plumber, so if you have any problems just give me a call," He hands Logan his business card "Harvey says you are coming to the match today, well hopefully we can impress you and maybe you can watch me score. I play upfront with Tony, well more like, I play alongside Tony, as he is the big shot in the team, well least he thinks he is. Well I guess I better get going I will catch you later."

Training the Team

That afternoon Logan got a taxi to the Dorchester FC, when he got to the ground there was security on the gate. Logan said that there was a ticket left for him. The security ushered Logan through. The ground had three grandstands, there was one either side of the goals and one on the right side of the pitch. On the left side there were a burger van and there was a few people walking around. Logan noticed in the stand, the policeman and Harvey's fiancée Sophie. He went up and sat next to them in the stand. Captain Rodgers spoke to Logan "Good afternoon, good to see you again Mr Logan."

He replied, "Thank you." He took his seat and could see the two teams warming up on the pitch. Captain Rodgers asked Logan, "How have you settled into Dorchester? I see that Harvey has been taking you around and showing you the town."

Logan then tells him "Yes Harvey has shown me round the town and introduced me to the town and helped me with finding my way around the town, it's funny how all the players in the team also have important vital jobs in the town."

The captain then said, "Yes most of the team all have important jobs in town. As we are an amateur team, they have to balance their work and football life. A little different to what you are used to, they don't earn mega bucks, they need to work to support their families." Then Logan saw a middle aged man and a young, slim, fit blonde hair woman, who was more focused on her phone than anything else, walking up to them. The gentleman then spoke to Logan, "Hello Mr Logan. My name is Mr Sharpe, I believe you have met my son, he is the star of this team. If it wasn't for him, this team would be crap and this lovely lady is my daughter, she is a famous tick book instafan or whatever it is called and has thousands of followers." She took her head from her phone and smiled and gave Logan a wink and he smiled back. Then Mr Rodgers said, "That's rich, your son isn't exactly a team player."

This made Mr Sharpe snap back, "My son is leader of the team, that's why your son follows him around, wanting to be him. Logan, I don't know why you are sitting with these commoners, a man of your stature should be up with me in the director's box, a star like you."

Logan said, "I am okay where I am, thank you. Maybe next time." Mr Sharpe then said "Well I would like to invite you to Sunday dinner at my house, it would be my pleasure to have you at my table. I can tell you about my plans for the town."

Logan said, "I have no plans Sunday, so it will be my pleasure to join you for Sunday dinner. See you then."

He watched as they headed over to the box. Logan couldn't take his eyes of Mary, Mr Sharpe's daughter. Sophie warned Logan, "I would stay away from her, she has reputation for being a bit of whore." Logan smirked at this and got himself comfortable for the match Mary watched him more than she watched what was happening on the pitch he noticed. The match kicked off and Logan was watched the game but every now again took a look over to see what Mary was doing. Dorchester were struggling in the match, they were already one nil down after fifteen minutes. They struggled to keep hold whole of the ball, every time they had it, they gave it away. Logan also noticed that whenever Tony got the ball often after he was passed to by

101

Rodgers. He tried to take on the opposition on his own and then lost the ball. Logan saw that Sophie was screaming and jumping out of her seat. Dorchester FC were two nil down by the thirty fifth minute of the first half. The team was low in confidence and before the end of the first half they conceded again. There was a player that shocked Logan, it was Tank. Whenever he kicked the ball, there was a lot of power behind it. Tank kicked the ball and it hit the opposition, launching the player in the air. Logan turned to the captain Rodgers and said, "Wow he put some welly behind that."

The captain responded with, "Yes, if he could learn to hit the target, he would be lethal."

Logan laughed, "Yes he just needs the right coach."

As they were three nil at the end of the first half Logan decided to get a cup of tea. He grabbed his tea and he took a seat at a bench, then a lady came and sat next to him. Logan recognised that it was the lady the one he sat next to on the bus. "Hello again."

As she sat next to him she then goes onto say to him. "So what do you think of the team?"

Logan looked at her and replied, "They are not the best team I have ever watched they need a little work."

The lady laughed and followed by saying, "Yes, it looks like they need someone who could just give them some advice and coaching. I don't suppose you know anyone who's free that could help them. Maybe someone who is staying in town while he waits for properties to sell."

There was a snigger from Logan. "Look I am flattered but I really am not interested, I just want to sell up. I'm not interested in getting involved. Look I don't plan on staying around any longer than I have too." The lady smiled. "Well I think that you're where you are meant to be, fate has brought you to Dorchester in the team's time of need and I would say it would be a shame if you couldn't help them with some of your knowledge. You have a choice, you can go back to your old life and carry on where you left of or you can write your own story in Dorchester the town will take care of you."

Logan looked at his tea but when he was going to speak back to her, she seemed to have disappeared. Logan returned to the stand and watched the second half. Dorchester ended up losing the match five nil. Logan said bye to the police captain and Sophie and waited for a taxi to take him to the pub.

When Logan arrived at the pub the team was already there, laughing and joking drinking. If he didn't know better he would have thought that they had won the match. Logan noticed that Tony was at the bar talking to Lucy, they were joking around and flirting together. Logan walked up to the bar but stopped in the middle of the pub and he got onto a chair and stood on it. He then shouted at the top of voice, "What the fuck is this? Are you celebrating losing? What a joke, you were embarrassing"

Tony then called out, "Wo wo wo I don't know who you think you are, but this is my team, not yours."

Harvey then says, "Logan is only speaking the truth."

Tony then turned to Harvey and said, "Might have known that you would be involved we have all seen you kissing his arse over the last few days, showing him round town, trying get him to come in and save the club. You have been trying to take back club from my family since my dad had to save it from your worthless dad. My dad has kept this club alive, while your dad has run it into the ground."

Logan then screamed. "Stop this, you are meant to be teammates not bickering like fucking children."

Tony said, "Look, no offence Logan, we don't need or want help from a washed-up a failure of a footballer, do we lads?" But Tony was surprised as the team, apart from Rover, said that well we could do with his advice to help the team and maybe we may be able to win a match. Tony stormed out followed, by Rover close behind. Logan addressed the team and said he would see them all Monday for training and to be prepared to work hard.

Logan then got a beer from Lucy, he then said to Lucy "You and Tony look quite cosy." she responded by angrily, saying that it had nothing to do with him but her and Tony have dated in the past. Logan finished his beer, then left the pub without speaking to Lucy.

The next day, Sunday, Logan dressed in his smartest shirt that he had and ordered a taxi to take him to Mr Sharpe's house. The house was a big stately home. Logan knocked and the butler opened the door and showed Logan into the drawing room. There, in the room was Tony, with Lucy and Mr and Mrs Sharpe and also Mary, who was on her phone again. "Welcome Logan, you have met my son, but this wonderful lady is my wife of many years, Claire. Now that we are all here shall we go into the dining room?"

As they were walked to the dining room, Logan pulled Lucy to one side and asked her. "Are you going to get back with Tony? He is such a tool.

She replied to Logan, "I am here as I am friend of Mrs Sharpe, not that I have to validate myself to you." She pushed his arm away and headed to the dining room. Logan sat next to Tony's sister. The meal was roasted chicken with all the trimmings.

Mr Sharpe spoke about his plans for the expansion of the superstore and how they were planning on building a new store.

Mr Sharpe loved to brag about his many business ventures and loved to show off how rich he was. Logan noticed thatat the other side of the table was Tony and Lucy they were joking around together.

During the mealLogan felt a hand around his crotch area and he realised that it was Tony's sister. She was just giving him a grin and licking her lips. Logan excused himself and asked where the toilet was. Logan left the table and went to the toilet, he didn't realise that he was being followed. As he entered the bathroom, Logan realised that Tony's sister was behind him. She followed him into the bathroom she closed and locked the door. She then launched herself on to him, kissing him. Logan tried to push her off when she told him. "Logan, I have seen how you have been looking at me, you know you want it and now let's get this big boy out and have some fun."

She moved her hand down and unzipped his flies and she moved her hand and pulled out his flaccid cock. She then put her mouth around his cock and started to suck, making it harder and firmer, until his cock was nice and firm. She then pushed him onto the toilet basin, slid her underwear to one side and sat herself on top of him, forcing his hard cock deep inside her. They had hard, quick sex, as he shot his load inside her, she jumped off him and repositioned her underwear before they returned to the dining table for desert, though Logan thought he hadalready had his. Once the meal had finished Logan thanked Mr and Mrs Sharpe for a lovely meal, he noticed that Lucy and Tony kissed each other goodbye. As Logan was leaving, Tony's sister came up to him and whispered in his ear, and said, "Call me, lover boy."

The next day Logan stopped off at the shop and brought eggs before he headed to Dorchester FC for training. The team were already warming up. Logan hadn't yet met the player coach Bob, he was also the town bus driver. Logan called him over and whispered in his ear.

They called over the rest of the team. "Okay team, now after watching you play the other day, your biggest problem is that you don't play as a team. Now, what I want you to do is, firstly, we are going to get rid of the ball (Logan then pulls out an egg from his pocket) and replaced itwith this egg. I want you to pass it around carefully, without breaking it, from one edge of the pitch to the other. You must work together."

Tony said, "This is stupid. I am not playing with egg."

Then player coach says. "Look Tony, let's humour him. What have we got to lose, let's hear him out."

Tony screamed. "Fine but this is fucking ridiculous." The team were given egg. it started with Harvey, who passed it onto Luke, who passed to Tom and then it reached Charles. The egg was working way round before Tony screamed, "Give it to me" Charles passed it to Tony but it missed Tony and end up hitting Rover on the head. The team all burst out laughing as the egg was dripping down from Rover's head. Logan pulled out another egg his pocket. Let's try this again, you need to work together to protect the egg. You must trust your teammates. If you can do this with the egg, then what wonders could you do with a ball." Tony then decided he had enough of training and walked off. Logan asked the coach to just go over his normal routine that he would normally do and so he can observe. The coach started taking the rest of team to doing some drills, Rover still had the remains of the egg on him. Logan followed Tony, caught up with him and called out his name.

Tony stopped, turned and said to Logan. "Look mate, let's get things straight. I am big deal around here, not you, I will still be here when you have gone back to London. No one here likes you, they just feel sorry for you. One more thing, stay away from Lucy. She is my girl and that is your only warning. This is my team not yours." Tony then carried on walking.

Later that evening when Logan was sitting in front of the TV at his uncle's cottage, there was a knock at the door. Logan answered it and there stood it was Harvey and his dad.

Harvey spoke to Logan. "Sorry to disturb you this evening but me and my dad have been talking. We were wondering while you were in town and waiting for stuff to happen, would you like to be the Dorchester Manager. It will be on a match by match contract and you can leave whenever you want, no strings attached."

Logan looked at them both. "If I become your temporary Manager, I want full say in the team and training and the players."

Harvey's dad then spoke up. "Yes, you will be in charge of the team As the chairman of the club, I want you to help the team. We need your help, the team can't work as a team, they struggle with the basics." Logan said, "you got yourself a deal."

He then laughed. Harvey asked him what was so funny Logan said, "I can't wait to see Tony's face when he sees that I am now his boss, oh this is going to be fun."

They shook hands and Harvey told Logan to come to the stadium tomorrow and he be will shown him the office.

The next day Logan arrived at the stadium and made his way to the manager's office. In the office was the player coach Harvey and his dad and the contract. Logan looked through the details and he said to them. "I just want to make sure that we are all understanding that this is not a permanent deal and once my business is done, I can leave I just am offering my services while I am in town." They all agreed on this Logan puts pen to paper and signs up. Bob the player coach then told Logan that their next match on Saturday was the first qualifying round in the FA cup. He had details of the opposition. Logan then asked Bob. "As I have only seen Dorchester play one match I would like to watch all their old matches so I can see the whole team's strength and weakness. Logan and Bob spent the whole day in the office watching old footage and coming up with tactics.

That evening all the team arrived but before they started training Bob made a speech, "Good evening lads, I would like to inform you that the club has hired Logan as temporary Manager. He has offered his services to help us while we are without a manager." The team all gathered around Logan and congratulated, him apart from Tony who said, "This isn't fair, you wait till my dad hears about this."

Logan then spoke up. "Look Tony, I think we have gotten off on the wrong foot. I am here to help the team, that's all I am not here to upset anyone. Let's say we start a fresh for the good of the Team."

Logan held out his hands to shake Tony's. Tony then told Logan. "I will go along with this for now. Just remember that I am the best player in this team, so don't even think about dropping me, as it will be the last thing you do." Logan replied. "I wouldn't dream of it. Now that's sorted, me and Bob have been looking at all your strengths and weakness, but before we can work on that we need to go back to basics."

He then pulls out another egg from his pocket. It took them ten eggs before they were able to pass the egg from one end of the pitch to the other without breaking it. The team were happy with their achievement by working together and trusting each other. Even Tony was shocked that they were able to complete this task. Logan then told the team that he would spend the rest of the week, in the build up to the cup match on working with each player to help them with their game.

After training Logan fetched some papers from the office but before he left, he saw Harvey out on his own, he was taking shots and goals. Logan was impressed with the accuracy of the shots but before he could go out and speak to him his taxi had arrived.

Logan that evening, went to the pub for a drink and a bite to eat. He found an empty table and laid out on the table each player's profile. Lucy brought over his dinner and a beer and said to Logan. "The word round the town is that you are going to work with Dorchester FC."

He looked up at her, smiled and said "Oh yes, I have a few plans for the team to help improve them."

Over the next few days Logan drew up some basic drills for Bob to go over to the team. Logan pulled The Tank to one side and asked him to follow. Tank followed Logan over to a wall. On the wall was a beer can and there was a football on the ground. "Now, Tank I have watched you and we need to work on your shooting accuracy with the shooting you have the power but power isn't everything."

Logan then kicked the ball and knocked the can of the wall. He then turned to Tank: "Your turn." Tank lined the ball up and he hits the ball it goes flying in the opposite direction from the can. Logan said, "Good try now let's try it again."

Tank tried five more times but was getting nowhere near the can. Tank became more and more frustrated. Logan said, "I want to try something." He put a blindfold over Tank's eyes. Tank shouted. "How am I meant to see the ball like this?"

Logan said to him. "Trust me, just hit the ball as hard as you can."

Tank then took two steps back and with all his power he smacked the ball and heard the sound of a can falling to the ground. Tank took his blindfold off and was shocked to see that he had done it. Logan said, "Try not to think of the target, as I can see this make you more nervous. Just trust yourself that you are going to hit the target. Now let's give it a go without the blindfold." Tank was practising hitting the can, he was hitting it almost every time, when he missed he would have another try. Logan could see the confidence building up in him.

Logan went tothe office after training. He saw Harvey doing shooting practise. Logan decided to sneak at peak at him. Logan sat and watched him for a few minutes and thought to himself, 'why Harvey is in goal, he should be scoring, not saving the goals.'

Harvey explained. "My family have kept goal since the club was formed by my great grandfather. My dad was keeper until he retired and I will pass this onto my children when I have them. It is my duty to carry on in goal."

Logan was shocked and coughed and under his breath said, "Bullshit," he then carried on with "Look Harvey, I have travelled Europe and played for a few clubs and seen and played with some great ballers and some shite ones. What I have seen here is, with the right coaching, you could be one of the good ones."

Harvey replied. "No offense Logan, but I am not outfielder, I am a goalkeeper, that is my role in the team nothing more needs to be said."

Logan was about to speak when Harvey screamed. "I am a keeper I am a keeper." He then kicked a football in frustration and he stormed off Logan watched as the ball as it soared into the air. It curved in mid-air and it ended up in the goal. Logan said under his breath said, "Holy shit, I need to get him upfront."

Over the next few days Logan continued to work on hitting the target with power and accuracy with Tank. He also noticed that Harvey no longer stayed around after training but one day after training he decided to follow him. Harvey was practising his shooting in secret and Logan decided to secretly film him.

The weekend came, it was the day of their first qualifying match in the FA cup they were playing Hemel Hempstead. The team were in the changing room getting ready for the match. Logan named his first line up for the match. Harvey in goal with Wise, Elliot, Tank, Tim Penfold, Rodgers, Brooks, Angelos Calvin Penfold, Sharpe and Mcfadden. He has said that he wanted to keep the team as it was and didn't want to make changes too soon. Logan told the team that Tank was to take the free kicks to Sharpe's displeasure. He was going to speak up but Rodgers nudged him and he decided to keep quiet for now.

The match was very slow, not many shots at goal. Both teams were having misplaced passes and neither team challenged the keepers during the first half. Tony wanted the ball passed to him but was then hanging onto the ball too much. During the half time break Logan addressed the team. "Look team we need to give the Tank a chance to unleash hell. So we need to work the ball to outside the area and draw a foul, then Tank can step up and with pure power smack the ball into the goal, even if the keeper can manage to get a finger to it, he will be unable to stop it from hitting the back of the net."

The second half was going the way of the first, a snore fest, then in the seventy seventh minute, Mcfadden was fouled just outside the area. Tony picked up the ball and was about to place it down for the free kick when Rodgers whispered into his ear.

He then said to Tank. "Come on then Tank, let's see what you got."

Tank placed the ball down and took four steps, back then he unleashed all his power on the ball. It flew through the air and over the wall. The keeper jumped but was unable to reach the ball and he could only watch as a ball flew past him into the goal. The team rushed to the Tank. He had put them in front. The match finished one nil.

The team celebrated in the bar. Even the local radio had it as breaking news that they had finally won a match. The team bought Tank lots of drinks as he was their star man. When Logan got to the pub, saw the team enjoying themselves. Tank was already pissed and slurring his words he wobbled over to Logan "eloo poach ev bid vell din she," he said to him, Logan grabbed his shirt, looked him straight in the eye and sai "It is time that you went home Tank."

Tony came up and said, "The night has only just started boss and Tank is the man don't be such a buzz kill." Logan angrily raised his voice so that the whole pub could hear him. "Now I'm all into celebrating, but I have learnt the hard way, playing and partying don't mix if you want to be winners. Now as I'm the coach I am going to set some ground rules:

Rule one if we lose, no one drinks.

Rule two if we win, each player may have two beers

Rule three if you don't like rule one and two then fuck off."

Tony was getting angry, he made a fist with his right hand and squared up to and got in Logan's face. Rodgers pulled him back and again whispered something in his ear. As Tony left, he said, "We will follow the rules but when you fail and have left, I will remain the star, this is my team and will always be my team, you are just warming the bench as a publicity stunt. No one will remember you when are gone or care." Logan then turned and grabbed a and drink from the bar.

After the cup match, they had a league match in the middle of the week. They drew this match nil nil. In the training session over the next week or so Logan decided to work with the Penfold twins on their passing. He started with having them directly in front of each other and passing the ball to each other. Each day Logan had them move further apart. Logan impressed on them that he wanted the twins to be able to pass the ball to each other, no matter where they were on the pitch. He wanted them to interchange positions and both of them be able to cross the ball into the box or take shot on the goal. They needed to be in sync at all times and be like a hive mind. Over the next two weeks they spent every minute they could passing the ball to each other, they were even practising passing the ball to each other between customers!at their shops. Even when they had a family gathering, and they were practised with their family.

One evening Logan was at the pub with Lucy. It was a dull quiet, night and the pub was empty. Logan saw that Lucy was struggling to stay awake. Logan then spoke to her. "Lucy, let's close up and go for a walk. It looks like you could do with some fresh air."

Lucy rubbed her eyes, then replied. "What about the pub? I can't just close up and go for a walk. What about the customers?" Logan looked around the pub and said, "What customers? Even the spiders have got bored and gone home." Lucy responded with "but…but…" Logan took her hand and put his middle finger put over her mouth, "As your boss, I am ordering you to come for a walk with me."

Lucy said, "Fine, as you're the boss." She went to grab her coat. They locked up the pub and they headed off to the local park for a walk. In the shadows Tony was lurking. He had a grin on his face, like he had some devilish plan.

Logan and Lucy found a park bench and sat down together. Lucy looked deeply into Logan's eyes, she was getting lost in them. It was as if they were drawing her in. It was a perfect evening. It was still light and it was so quiet. Lucy broke the silence by saying "I just can't figure you out, one minute I think you are a complete jerk, then next minute, I find that there is something special about you and I want to know more."

Lucy hadn't noticed that Logan was no longer looking into her eyes but he was watching some kid doing tricks with a football in the park. "Sorry did you say something?" he asked. She responded, "Never Mind."

Then Logan asked Lucy. "Who's the kid and why isn't he in my team." Lucy looked over at the kid doing the tricks. The nerd. That's the doc's son Corey. The doc said he is going to off to Uni in a few years and study to be a quack like his dad. He is nothing but a bookworm, he's always got his head in books, he is no baller." Before Lucy could even finish, he was already on his way over to him. He called over to him. "Hey kid, good skills." The kid saw Logan and ran off. Logan did tried to chase after, him but couldn't catch up with him.

While Logan was chasing after him Tony had arrived in the park, and walked over to Lucy and sat on the bench He told Lucy, "Lucy, I am telling you this as a friend and I don't want to see you get hurt. He is using you, so he can get into your knickers. He couldn't give a fuck about the town, it's all an act. You and the town will realise when he finally sells up and fucks off, leaving you behind."

Lucy responded with "He isn't the guy that papers report him to be, there is more to him than that."

114

Tony with his voice raised a little louder said "Look Lucy, I care about you deeply and I'm sorry for cheating on you, Logan is worse than me, he will fuck and run. He has already fucked my sister, they fucked when we had the meal together. Logan is only interested in getting as much pussy as he possibly can. It was once reported that he was working his way round take away menu." Lucy was wiping her eyes, as she had tears coming from them. Logan came back, over panting from chasing after the kid. Tony nodded and smiled at Logan and walked off. Logan could see that Lucy wasupset, he tried to touch her. She pushed him away. he then asked "Are you okay? What's the matter?" Lucy screamed out "Why don't you ask his sister what's the matter?" she pushed past him and walked away, still rubbing her eyes from the tears running down her face.

It was day before their second qualifying game in the FA cup.Itwas away game and they were travelling to Dover. The coach was waiting to take the team to the game, the team were waiting for tony and Rodger, as they were the last two to arrive. The Penfolds were practising their passing around the car park, they were kicking the ball over the cars and even over the bus. No matter where they were, they were able to pick out each other. Tony turned up in a new red Chevrolet Corvette C8 car, with the radio blaring away. He swung the car into a space, just missing the twins. They yelled "Watch where you are fucking going."

A few of the players went over to look at his new car, 'wow' and 'cool' could be heard. Logan said "Nice of you to join us, now let's get on the coach and get going." Tony replied with "Woh there, me and double R are going to get in my present from my dad and drive ourselves up. No offence but that coach looks like it is being held together with tape and chewing gum. I don't think it will make it to the end of the road, let alone to Dover. So

115

we have decided to travel in style."

Logan angrily called out to them, "I don't think so we are a team and should travel as a team so we can go over any final preparations."

Tony wasn't listening. He had turned up his radio even louder, he then closed the door of the car and revved the engine and spun the car out of the space and in flash it was off. Logan was screaming at the car but it was already out of the car park and it was gone. Logan turned to the rest of the team and yelled "Get on the fucking coach and let's get going."

The coach trip was quiet with just the radio playing Logan was scribbling down on paper and was working on his team sheet for the game.

The team arrived in Dover and went into the changing room. Tony and Rodger were already there. They were sitting in the 'away team' changing room with big smug faces. Tony called out with "What has taken you so long?"

Logan walked over to Tony and yelled in his face, "Don't you ever fucking do that again, we travel together as a team."

Tony came back with "A team! Look Logan, what do you know about this team? You think just because you win one match and Mr Smih is sucking up to you, like you, are some fucking football God but really everyone knows that you are just another fucking loser, like the rest of them."

Logan replied with "These are your teammates, you need to show them respect, now leave the changing room because you are dropped."

Tony started laughing then said "Wo wo not so fast boss (laughing when he said boss). Just like you have a percentage in the club, my dad also has percentage in the club and another present that he gave me was a new contract and in the terms it

116

states that under no circumstances can I be dropped and my name is the first on the team sheet."

Logan shouted back, "What the fuck, I was told that I had say in the team?"

Tony again laughing in his face, "You can pick the rest of the team but unless I am injured, my name will always be on the team sheet. If you don't like it then there's the door and we go back to the way things were before you came and started messing around."

Logan turned around and screamed,"Fucking hell."

He walked over and hits the wall he then yells at Bob, the assistant, to come over. They sat in the corner of changing room they were then discussing the team. There was a knock at door, it was the referee's assistant, he wanted the team sheet for the starting line-up Logan handed over a piece of paper, turned to Tony and gave him a wink.

He huddled the team together and began to write the starting line-up on the whiteboard. Smith in goal, Wise as left back, Elliot and Champman as centre backs, Tim Penfold as right back, Calvin Penfold right midfield, Angelos and Brooks in midfield, Glass as left midfield, Sharpe and Mcfadden up front.

Once Logan had finished writing the team sheet Tony piped up, "What the fuck! Up with that why has Double R been dropped, he is my swing man, he is my assist master. You have no clue to what you are doing, you have just done this to get back at me. You're such a douche."

Logan responded with, "I have no idea what you are talking about. I am doing what is best for the team. This has nothing to do with you, but if you don't like it, then there the door." It was Tony's time to strop off he kicked a water bottle which bounced of the wall and just missed hitting Rover.

Rover then shouted out, "This isn't fair. I want to play." Bob the coach went over to Rover, and sat him down and calmed him down.

The match against Doverstarted slowly. Dover had few shots atgoal but nothing that really challenged Smith in goal. Tank had a couple of free kicks, but none that were in a good area but then in the forty forth minute of the match. Tim found Calvin in good space for a launching pass. Calvin was on the right of the box, he saw that Mcfadden wasfree he passed the ball to him and all he had to do was tap the ball into the back of net. Onenil! It was up just before half time the team celebrated with Mcfadden, but Logan knew that the twins were the real key to that goal. The whistle went for half time and Logan may sure that he went over to the twins and made sure they knew their impact on the game.During the second half, Dover had stepped up their attack. They were trying everything they could to get an equaliser. Logan saw that Wise was fast when he ran from the defence with the ball and nobody could catch him, but when he got into the opposition half he seemed to freeze and was tackled, returning the ball to Dover. In the fifty sixth minute there was another seeking pass, this time it was Calvin who found Tim and just like the first half Tim passed and found Tony in space he hits the ball but it was a not a good shot, a grass cutter, butthe keeper missed it and it slipped past the keeper and Dorchester were now two nil up. Tony was celebrating as he had just scored a wonder goal. In the sixty first minute, Glass went down with injuries. Rodgers got up from the bench and started to warm up but Logan looked at Hughes and then says to him,"Warm up, you're going on kid.them what you can do." To Rodger's dismay, the young Hughes went on in place of Glass, Rodgers sat back down sulking. The match ended two nil. On the way back, on the coach, the team were in jubilant mood after thewin. They sang songs, even Bob was singing they sank a song "Bob the Bus Driver he's our man. Bob the Bus Driver can he drive it? Yes hecan."

Suddenly the coach had to swerve as it was undercut Bob Screamed at the other driver then the realised who it was. It was Tony in his new car. They carried on until they arrived back in town.

The team left the coach and they headed off to the pub Logan was left on the coach sitting on his own. Bob turned from the driver's seats and said "Hey boss, you okay? We won, so why do you look sad?" Logan replied, "I'm okay Bob, just thinking to myself."

Bob then came back with, "Okay boss. Well, if you don't mind, I've got get the coach back to depot and then I need to get my bus for the night as I am working the night bus."

Logan then asked him "Bob, hope you don't mind, me asking but how many hours do you work with the team and driving the busses."

Bob laughed "Well, let's just say I don't have free time since my dad ended up with dementia and had to be moved into a care home. I had to give up my dream of being a formula one driver and get a real job to help pay for his care. I was offered the player coach job here on a part time basis and being the town's main bus driver, so couldn't refuse to turn it down. My dad is living in the local care home and he is happy. So, I still get drive for living, it's just a little slower than I would like, but it pays the bills."

Logan looks at him and said "You are a good man Bob, a truly good man to give up your dream to help family." Bob nodded and then said "Good night boss."

Logan decided not to go the pub that evening and headed straight to his uncle's cottage. The next day Logan went to the

119

estate agents to find out if there had been any enquires about the two properties. Mr Brooks and his son were both there. They said that, as yet, they had not had any interested in either property's they said that they would let him know if there were any offers.

That evening, as there was no training, Logan decided not to go the pub but decided to go to one of the neighbouring towns. Hetook the bus. Bob was the driver and greeted him with "Evening boss. Logan asked about the best town to go to in the evening. Bob said he knew the perfect place and Logan jumped on board.

Logan spent the day shopping in town and as the day drew to a close, henoticed a bar, similar to the Dorchester pub. Logan went in for a drink. He hadn't noticed the sign saying 'Drag night'. The bar was busy. There was a rowdy bunch cheering and booing there was already a drag artist singing. Logan went to the bar and to order a beer. He sat on a bar stool, the barman said, "You're not one of the regulars."

Logan looked at him and came back with "I was just passing through and thought I would grab a beer before heading home. The singing is very entertaining." The barman said that the town had been holding a drag night for over two years. The next artist came on, she played the piano and sang the song 'Girls just want to have fun' to the audience. The crowd cheered her. A table with a group of men. They were heckling the drag artist after she had finished her song. She started to talk to the audience and she told some jokes about being a drag artist. The table of hecklers became more abusive with their heckles. It wasn't until the artist decided to interact with them. She pulled up a chair and sat in between the loudest one of the groups, "Well it looks like a town is missing it's idiots."

This annoyed them. The loudest of the group said, "Look

nonce, we are just here to have a good time. Why don't you prance yourself back on stage and sing for us? That's what you'repaid to do isn't it sissy boy?"

The drag artist was pissed off with this comment and she grabbed a beer from the table and then poured it over his head. He and his mates then stood up and surrounded the drag artist. Then one of the group pushes him. Logan watched this from the bar. He didn't like what he saw and he left the bar and headed over to the group and he then stood in front of them.

He spoke to the group's leader, "Now boys, I think it is time you called it a night. I suggest you head back to your home and leave this entertainer to get on with her show."

The shortest member of the group the piped up with "Wo, look, it's Logan. Wow. Can I have your autograph?"

Then the loudest one of the group the spoke up "Look, I don't know what some washed up failure of footballer is doing here, unless maybe you're another bum fucking faggot." Before anyone else spoke the bar manager came over and said, "I think it is time you left. Now you've had your little bit of fun but you are spoiling the night for everyone else."

A man, who was slightly overweight said to the group, "Come on guys, let's not spend any more money in this shit hole. If we stay here any longer, we may catch the gay disease."

They pushed past the three of them and barged their way out of the pub.

The drag queen thanked Logan for his help but when turned to look at the drag artist, he heard the words "Holy shit Boss, I can explain.," But before Logan could respond, the artist ran to the back of the stage area. The next artist came to the stage. Logan headed back to the bar, ordered another beer and waited for the end of the show. Logan saw that Mateo was trying to

121

sneak off, he had a duffle bag over his shoulder, trying to hide. Logan called to him. Mateo tried to make out that he hadn't heard him and headed to the door, when he felt a hand on his shoulder. As he turned he saw that it was Logan. Mateo started to cry and said "I'm so sorry boss, if you want to fire me, I understand."

Logan replied with "No, why would I fire you? You're one of the team's best players."

Mateo was shocked at this "What do you mean? Surely you won't want me in your team, I'm a Drag artist for fuck's sake. Aren't you worried how this will affect the team? If this ever got out that I am one of the top drag artists."

Logan pointed to the chair and urged Mateo to sit down. The sa down at a table and Logan spoke with a reassuring voice. "Mateo, I am not here to judge you. What you do on your day off is up to you mate. I am big supporter of the LGBT community."

Mateo came back with, "Oh I'm not gay. I am very much straight and I have recently got married and am expecting my first child."

Logan said congratulations then Mateo carry on talking "There are two sides to me. Side one is the shop worker and part time footballer and then there's my alter ego, Martha the Drag queen."

Logan asked how he got into drag. "I have always wanted to be on stage and when I was at drama school I came up with Martha. Once I finished at drama school, I started doing some local gigs in my town, then one evening my dad was drinking in the pub that I was performing at and when he saw it was me,he got on the stage and beat me to within an inch of my life. I ran away from home and bought myself a one-way ticket to the end of the bus line. I ended up in Dorchester I met your uncle and he told me about a place that I could stay and told me about getting a jon at the local supermarket. After a few months of living in Dorchester. I was in your uncle's bar and there was a flyer for Drag artist competition. I entered and won and ever since I have been performing in towns but have made sure that I don't perform in Dorchester I don't think the team will understand."

Logan smiled at him and to Mateo's amazement said "Well, as your manager, I say that you shouldn't be ashamed of who you are and if anyone on the team has a problem with that, then tell them to come and see me. Look Mateo, maybe if your two parts became one part, you could become a better all-round player. As you are never truly giving your full self."

Mateo then responded with, "Look boss, there's no way I can tell my teammates about this and now that you have found I will stop performing and Martha will retire."

Logan lent forward and then spoke up, "Mateo, how does your wife feel about you doing this? Does she know?"

"Yes, my wife knows. We met at drama school and she helped me come up with Martha. She understands that I am a true performer and I love to entertain.She normally comes to all my shows but due to her pregnancy wasn't able to get to this one. She is the only person who knows the true me and apart from you and my dad who I haven't spoken to in years, are the only other ones who know and I would like to keep it that way."

"Okay, your secret is safe with me and look, as far as I'm concerned you can carry on being Martha, I am no Simon Cowell but you are a good singer, best act of the night."

Mateo smiled stood up, gave Logan a hug and thanked him. He said as he was leaving that would see him at training.

Over the next few weeks, the team had couple of league games. Theyhad a couple of draws but no wins, they had not yet been able to bring cup form to the league games.

One training session Logan Wise called over Wise over. Logansaid that he was going to take him somewhere to help him to be better player. He said that he had noticed that he has lots of speed but when he reached the other half, it was as if he ran out of ideas and didn't know what to do. Logan had booked a taxi which picked up him and Wise, who was still dressed in his training gear.

The rest of the team were puzzled and wondered where he had taken Wise. Then Rover and Tom then piped up with, "Looks like someone is getting fired or they're going out for a little bum action."

The rest of the team where not impressed with this and turned away and headed off todo there training drills with Bob.

Logan and Wise arrive at the school. Wise looked at Logan and asked, "Why are we here, I hated school and don't intend to go back and the food is bloody shite."

Logan t responded with, "We aren't here to go to class and I will only make you eat the food if you don't do what I ask of you."

Logan then took him to track and field. Then Logan spoke to Wise, "I have been watching you during the matches and you have all the speed but when you reach the other half, it's like you have run out of ideas. So I want you to forget the rest of the drills and over the next week, I want you to come here I want you to run the full length of running track and, as you may have noticed,there is a football pitch and there's a goal in the middle of the field. When you have run the course, I want you to then hit the ball to me for me to score. I want you to imagine that you are running into space and then hitting the ball into striker to score. Then the second drill I want is I have also observed that for all your speed you have you are unable to control the ball when running into space, So the second drill I want you to practise is, running the track with the ball at your feet without losing control. Now let's get started."

Wise ran as fast as he could around the running track. As he came round to the end, where the ball was, he was running out of breath and as he reached the ball.He stopped then he kicked the ball. It went soaring in the air, but it was nowhere near where Logan was standing. Logan then shouted to him to try again. He then ran around again, panting away. As he got to the end there was another ball ready for him. He stopped running and then hits the ball. Again it landed nowhere near Logan, it was actually further away than the last try. Logan walked over and said, "Wise, why do you stop and then hit the ball? Why don't you try and kick it when you are running. It's like when you stop you are over thinking the cross. Well let's try the other drill. Let's see how well you run with the ball and your speed."

Wise again got himself ready and then he started to run with the ball at his feet. He didn't get far before he lost control and the ball ran away from him. He then tried again and the same thing happened. He tried to do it for the third time and again he lost control. He was growing frustrated and angry with himself.

Logan comforted him and then spoke to him with these words, "Wise, you are probably the fastest person I have met and if you can practise this and learn to control the ball at speed there will be no one who will be able to get anywhere near you."

Wise looked at him and came back with "I will try boss. I will make sure when I am not cooking I will be up here and practise."

Logan then patted him on the back and smiled and then said "This team is on the verge of greatness."

Wise laughed before their taxi arrived. When they were in

125

the car Wise looked at Logan and said "Hey boss, can I ask you a question?"

Logan turned and replied "Of course, anytime, ask away."

"Why do you not drive and get taxi and busses all the time?" Logan then responded with "Well it has been well documented that after my career ended that I didn't take it well and I started drinking a lot and one evening I had been thrown out of nightclub and rather than get the taxi home I got into my car and was driving round London and I was swerving all over the road and I was spotted by the police who try to pull me over but rather than pull over I made off and ended up crashing into another car head-on when trying to escape. After this I was banned from driving and hefty fine and since then I have never got behind a wheel of car again."

"Fair enough boss."

Logan spent the evenings working with Wise on his speed. Day by day he was getting better and controlling the ball when running and he was able, by the end of the week, he was able to put a ball into the box for Logan to head into the goal.

During the evenings Logan tracked down the lad he had seen doing tricks in the park. He had spoken to Harvey about him and where he would likely be able to find him. Harvey said that normally, if he wasn't in the library, he would be at his dad's surgery, as his dad would have him there to learn and observe him. Logan spent most of the week staking out the library. It finally paid off on the Wednesday of that week. He watched as the one they called. The Nerd went into the library. Logan followed him and he watched as he saw that he went to the sport section. He then went over to the science area and sat at a table.

Logan then sat at his table the lad tried to make out that he didn't notice him. Logan looked at the book that he was reading.

126

The human body was the title also Logan noticed that every now and again the nerd was looking up at another table where there was a short little young lady with dark black hair with glasses also reading a book.

Logan decided to break the silence and with his most quiet voice, as he was in library, he asked "So what are you reading sport?"

The lad popped his head over the book and looked up. When he saw Logan he quickly tried to close the book and was got up to leave. Logan then said, "Woah, what is the rush mate? Just want to chat, no harm, no foul."

When the Nerd had been in rush to get away and tried to close the book, Logan had noticed that inside the human body book, there was another book. Logan then with a louder voice asked, "So what are you really reading?" The Nerdagain panicked quickly tried to get up but the book that was hidden fell to the floor. Logan bent down and picked it up and noticed that it was a football skills book. Logan smiled said "Now that a good book." The Nerd panicked and said it isn't mine, I promise." Logan put his hand on the nerd's shoulder and said "Look mate, let's have a little chat. Maybe if you help me out,I can help you out with your little girlfriend over there that you're stalking." The Nerd looked slightly embarrassed at this and said, "No, it isn't like that, we just both like going to the library." Logan responded with "Look mate, I just want to talk." The Nerd sat himself back down and told Logan "Okay, we will just talk, that is all."

Logan said, "I saw you the other day doing your tricks, you have some skill, sorry I don't know your name everyone who I have asked about you they just call you the Nerd or the Doctor son."

The lad laughed and replied, "Laugh out loud most people

in this town think I'm invisible and they don't pay much attention to me. My real name is Samuel Paige. So Mr Logan, what is you want to talk about?"

"Okay, I will get straight to the point. I saw you the other day and thought to myself that this kid has skill and would fit in nicely in the team, so why isn't he playing for Dorkchester FC and kid you better have a good reason."

Then Samuel looked up and very nervously said "It is my dad he wants me to go onto be a doctor like him. My family have always been the town's and the clubs doctor. It is expected that I continue to represent my family in the town I am expected to go to uni to study and when my dad retires, I will take over. I have not got time to play ball."

Logan, under his breath, said "Bullshit look Sam, I am not one to stand in anybody's way. If you want to be a doctor and help the town with their warts and cock rash, then that's fine by me, but you will also be wasting some god given talent I reckon. You have the ability to play well, not quite top flight football like me, but I can see lower league in your future if you let me coach you and join my club. Look, I have a part time contract."

He pulled out some paper from his pocket. Sam was taken back with this "Look Logan, I appreciate you coming to find me but I am no footballer, I will be a doctor one day."

Just as they were about to continue speaking, the young girl that Sam had been watching, got up from her table and walked past and said "Hi Sam" Sam stuttered back with "Hi Mi- Mi- Mi- Miranda."

But the time he said Miranda, she had already left, Logan had a big smirk on his face and said "Well, well, Mr Nerd has a crush. I tell you, if you join up with me for the rest of the season, I will get you a date with Mi Mi Mi Miranda."

Sam sheepishly said "She won't want to go out with a loser like me. She is so beautiful and wonderful. Her smile can melt a thousand hearts."

Logan pretend to gag and came back with, "Look, you clearly like that girl and if you trust me, I will not only coach you on football but also, I will coach you in how to get the woman."

Sam looked up and said, "Okay, let's just say I join your team and let you help me. My dad won't like it. What are we going to do about him? Logan again laughed and with another chuckle said, "Leave that to me."

Sam agreed to join Logan's team he signed the contract that Logan had brought for him. Logan informed him that training would be that night at seven forty-five, as they had a league game at the weekend to get ready for.

Sam arrived at seven forty-five sharp but there wasn't anyone else apart from Logan at the training ground. Sam asked Logan, "Where is everyone?" else Logan then told him that he wanted him to come before the rest of the team as he had a surprise for him. He pulled out a black, full-face mask and threw it at him and said, "I wanted you to join me before anyone else got here so I can give you your mask." He then said "This should stop your dad from finding out that you're playing football."

When the rest of the team arrived the changing rooms, Logan and Sam where already sat on the benches. Logan addressed the team. "Hi guys, I would like to introduce you your newest teammate Sam. Unfortunately he has a face that only mother would love So he has to wear a mask at all times. Now enough chit chat, let's get training, we have a league match to get ready for."

They went outside and started running their drills with Bob

and Logan.

The weekend arrived and the team were about to play their league match. The match was locked at nil nil. The game was reached the sixty eight minute. When Logan called over to the bench and told Sam to warm up as he was going on at the next break in play. The ball went out of play, the board was held up and it was showing Tony's number. When Tony noticed that it was his number was being shown up, he was furious. At first, he tried to make out that he didn't see the board, then Rodger called to him that his number is up.

Finally, after a few minutes he stormed off the pitch. He turned to Logan and said, "You will regret this. Nobody subs me off, ever."

He barged into Sam as he walked onto the pitch. Sam had a great debut for the team, he scored the winning goal and the team had finally won a league match.

The team spent the next week getting ready for their next FA cup qualifying round this was the third round after a week of drills, and Wise spent all that time working with Sam putting in the ball for him and setting the ball up for him.

On match day the team readied themselves for the game. When Mateo entered the changing room, he noticed that there was a ballet dress hanging from his bench peg and a newspaper below. He looked puzzled at this and walked over to his bench. He moved the dress and picked up the paper and the headline read DRAG FOOTBALLER playing for Dorchester. Tears randown his Mateo's face,he turned and ran out of the ground but before he did he screamed at Logan, "I trusted you with my secret."

Tony Laughed and said in the corner saying under his

breathe "Ah, what a shame. The little batty boy has left the club."

Logan heard this and turned and stood on the table and at the top of his voice shouted,"This was you wasn't it? You little prick. Why would you do this to your teammate?"

Tony responded with "I have no idea what you're talking about. How is my fault that we have a cross dressing faggot in our team? The team is better off without him and his gayness." Logan said "What the fuck! I haven't heard something so ridiculous in my fucking life."

Tony stood face to face with Logan and said "Look I don't understand what your problem is. I am the star of the team and I am the only one you should be worrying about, not that loser."

Logan then screamed, "Get the fuck out of here. You have no respect for your teammates. You think that you're some big shot player but really your're just shit. You make out you're the town's big shot just because you appeared in a calendar. What was the calendar the fugliest people around? Now, if you don't piss off I promise I will smack that smile of your face."

Tony was shocked at Logan's response. "Look calm down. I have done the team a favour. Look, we don't want some queer in our team. We don't want to be bum rushed in the changing room." Before Tony knew what had hit him, Logan had smacked him in the mouth and knocked him to the floor and at the top of his voice said "Look, you fecking homophobe. Get out of the changing room. People like you are what's wrong with the world. You don't care who you step on to get to the top." As Tony picked himself of the floor he tried to punch Logan, but Tank stepped in front of him. Tony backed off. seeing Tank in front of him. Tony then called out, "Well, I don't want to play for shit team. Youare not good enough to have me in your team. I am a star and should be playing for a team of stars not losers like you. But mark my

131

words, you will be sorry. I will make you pay, all of you will be sorry. Come on double R, lets go."

Rodger stepped forward and to Tony's shock he said, "I am staying, this is my team, You went too far this time, you hurt my friend and teammate."

Tony replied. "Well, I hope you're happy with the rest of these loser." Tony then stormed out of the changing room not looking back.

Once Tony had left Logan said"Well, now that he has left get ready for this is cup match."

Logan wrote the starting line-up for the match.

The team was Smith in goal, Wise, Elliot, Champman, Tim Penfold in defence, Rodgers, Brooks, Smith, Calvin Penfold, Hughes, Mcfadden up front.

Logan saw that Sam was a little disappointed that he wasn't starting but Logan came over and sat next to him. "Hey kid, what troubling you?" Sam turned to Logan and handed him a letter. Logan asked what this was Sam told him to read it. Logan looked at the letter and it was from the university and unfortunately Sam had not been given a place. It stated that 'Due to his grades they couldn't offer him a place'.

Sam then told Logan "My dad is going to be so disappointed in me, how can I face him?"

Logan said, "I am sure if you tried your best, he will be proud of you. Is there a way of resitting the test again," Sam snapped back with "Logan, no offence but you don't understand. It is my duty to continue the family legacy. The reason I spent so much time in the library and why I earnt the nickname Nerd is because unlike football which seems to have come naturally to me and I don't need to work on it, the science stuff I struggle to understand and this means I have to study twice as hard as everyone else and work that much harder so that I can make my dad happy. This will kill him knowing I've failed. What am I even doing playing football, I should be studying?"

Logan spoke in gentle voice "Look kid, I know what it is like to have a pushy parent but maybe this is blessing."

Sam snapped back with "A fucking blessing! This is your fault."

Logan responded with "Look, hear me out. I don't know much about science shit but I know football and you have some real talent. Let me talk to your dad and maybe I can make him understand that being a doctor is not where your future is."

Sam again shouted back to Logan "No don't talk to my dad. I promise I will continue to play for you if you promise not to tell my dad. I will have to see if I can make up the grades and reapply but you must never tell my dad or I will quit."

Logan said "Look I am not going to blackmail you and I promise I won't talk to your dad, I will leave that to you when you fill you are ready to tell him. I won't interfere."

Sam hugged Logan, thanked him and said he was sorry for saying it was his fault and he hadn't meant it, he had really been enjoying being a part of the team but he reminded Logan that he had promised him that he would help him with his girl troubles. Logan smiled and told him that to meet him on Saturday in the pub and they could discuss the issue.

The team had a great match the practise that Wise had been doing had really helped him. He ran up and down the left wing all game, putting really good balls into the box and in the twenty eighth minute he crossed the ball in that was headed in by Mcfadden. In the thirty third minute the Penfold brothers worked well and passed the ball across the box for Mcfaden to slide in and get his second goal. The team where buzzing by half time. The team were in jubilation. Logan calmed them down and said that they mustn't be complacent in the second half and carry on what we are doing. Logan then said he was going to make a change at half time and was taking off Hughes and bringing on Sam. Logan said to Sam, Forget about impressing your dad, just go and have some fun."

The second half carried on pretty much as the first half Dorchester were dominating the ball, in the fifty sixth minute Sam had been played a ball by Wise, he was one on one with the keeper. He looked around, but rather than placing in the back of the net, he passed the ball along to McFadden, who scored his first ever club hat trick. He ran over and gave Sam a hug. lifting him off the ground. In the end the other team scored a consolation goal and the game finished three one. After the game as the team left, McFadden approached Logan and invited him to dinner, at his house this evening to celebrate with his wife Emma and their son would love it if he came. Logan said that it would be a pleasure.

That evening Logan dressed smart, for the evening he had picked up a bottle of wine and a bunch of flowers. Logan knocked on the door of McFadden's house. When the door opened, Logan noticed a small boy standing at the door. The boy looked up at him and when he saw Logan, he ran off.

McFadden came round at saw Logan standing there.

"Come in!" he said to him.

Logan wiped his feet on the door mat and walked into the house. McFadden ushered him into the living room. McFadden's wife, Emma was in the kitchen, she called out hello. Logan responded and said hello back. Logan could see the boy peeping round the kitchen the door. Logan said hello and then the boy hid back round the door. McFadden said to Logan "Grab a seat, dinner isn't quite ready."

Logan sat in the armchair. The boy appeared then came up and stood in front of Logan. Logan noticed that boy had Down's Syndrome. Logan said, Hello there, and what is your name?" But when Logan spoke to him, he ran off and hid in the kitchen. McFadden sat next to Logan and passed him a beer and then said to Logan, "Sorry, he is a little bit shy. We don't tend to have many visitors. People don't know how to act round Rex, they don't see a child they just see his disability. So we tend to keep ourselves to ourselves."

Emma called out that dinner was ready. Logan and McFadden got up and went into the dining room. Rex was already sitting at the table. Logan gave him a smile and Rex smiled back. Mrs McFadden brought out the meal, it was spaghetti and meatballs, with garlic bread. Logan said that it smelled and looked very tasty and can't wait to get stuck in.

Logan was enjoying the meal, and he looked and saw that Rex was struggling to get the spaghetti on his fork. Logan turned to him and says "Look I show a little trick to twisting the spaghetti."

He put his fork in the middle of his plate and started to turn the fork, wrapping the spaghetti onto his fork and once there was enough of it, he lifted it off the plate. He showed it to Rex and said you try. Rex copied what Logan had done and he managed to get some spaghetti on his fork. There was a smile and jubilation on his face. He said, "Look Mum, I did it I did all by myself."

Mr and Mrs McFadden both praised Rex for what he had done. Mrs McFadden turned to Logan and said "Thank you, most people look at Rex and treat him as if he is stupid and isn't able to do anything himself. Most people would have tried to feed him and this would frustrate him even more. He loves to be independent."

Logan was enjoying his meal. Mrs Mcfaden spoke to Logan, "The team are doing so much better since you came and started coaching the team. It has also impacted on my husband, he isn't so grumpy when he gets home from matches. He's almost bearable to live with."

They all laughed. Logan then asked, "How did you end up in this town. What brought you here?"

Mrs McFadden replied, "When we lived in the city, Rex was struggling with his autism and struggled with loud noises whenever we were shopping. He would have melt downs. David was working all the hours to pay the bills at home and was struggling with work/life balance. With dealing with Rex's medical care Our marriage was struggling, we were always arguing. Then, out of the blue, David gets a phone call offering him a job in Dorchester. At first, I wasn't impressed about packing up and moving to the middle of nowhere. I was worried how this would affect Rex.

But this has been the best thing that has happened to us as a family. The small town life has really helped Rex, the quiet town life has really done wonders. He has less outbursts."

Logan asked why he hadn't seen Rex at any of their matches. David told him that due to the autism, Rex really struggles with sounds. They felt that taking him to a football match would be too much for him, so Rex had never seen his dad play, as they felt he wouldn't be able to cope with it. Logan said he may have someone who could help with this and to leave it with him and he said to all three of them that Rex will be able to see his dad play. Rex smiled and he jumped downfrom the table and got a ball it was the match ball from the game today as David had scored a hat trick he had been awarded the ball.

Logan said "Yes, your dad was amazing today he scored three great goals."

Rex tried to give Logan the ball saying, " Your ball, your ball."Logan said to him that it was his dad's ball, but Rex said, "No your ball."Logan took the ball from Rex and smiled. David then told Logan "Rex is correct. I would like you to have my match ball today, if it wasn't for you I would never have scored a hat trick. Me and the team are playing so much better with you as our coach. Each and every one of us have seen improvements and we know that you are only staying for a short while, so I would like you to have the ball to remember this moment."

Then his phone buzzed, he had received a message, he turned to Logan and said, "Boss, we have Foxford in the next round of the cup and you will never guess who has only gone a joined our rivals." Logan thought for a moment, then in a lightbulb moment, came up with the idea. "Tony has joined them." "Well least I don't have to drop him now. Oh well, no great loss."

The evening ended and Logan thanked the family for a lovely meal and a wonderful evening. He reminded them that he would help so that Rex will be able to come and see his dad play football.

At the teams next training session the team were all a buzz about having to play Foxford in the cup and also to get one over on Tony for leaving. Then the changing room went quiet as Tank walked in and he had a plaster across his face. Rodger broke the silence and said "What the hell happened to you?"

Tank then replied, "Oh this is nothing. I got it from my wrestling match last night and in reward I got a nice gold belt."

He chuckled to himself. Logan then came over to him. Tank looked a bit worried as he thought that he was going to get a bollocking. But instead he asked Tank when his next match was and to get the whole team tickets and they would support him. Boo his opposition and cheer for the champ. Tank gave Logan a hug, lifting him off the ground and told him that he was the best coach they had ever had at Dorchester, then apologised to Bob. Bob just gave a huge laugh and nodded in agreement. Logan and Bob then went through the training plans for this week stating that the team need to focus on the league before the Foxford and the biggest match in the club's history as they have never been in the FA cup proper.

Logan instructed the team to focus on the match. Logan had noticed that Mateo wasn't present. He asked the team if anyone had seen or spoken to him since the cup match. Brooks said that he had texted but had no response. He had tried to call but nothing his wife had spoken to Mateo's wife, but she said that Mateo had locked himself away in his mancave and hasn't left. He was not eating, speaking to his wife just becoming withdrawn. Logan told the team that he would speak to him and get him back to the team. He said, "But for now we need to get back to training." Logan h' asked the Penfold twins and Brooks to stay with him while Bob took the rest of the team to run drills.

"Okay Brooks, I have asked the Penfolds to stay with us, because they are going to pass the ball between them. I want you to read the ball and intercept their pass. I want you to practise knowing where the ball is going to go and be ready. The Penfolds are the attack if they score, they get five points. If you can get the ball off them, you get five points."

Logan watched as Brooks and the Penfolds were playing out his drill. At first the Penfolds were getting the better of Brooks, they had got fifteen points before Brooks managed to get the first interception. But once he had done it the first time, he managed to get to the score fifteen points each.

Logan walked over to them before they did their next drill. Logan said, "It looks like you're getting the hang of this. It's like you can see the pass before it happens, you're like Kante. Well, keep practising but also what I want you to do is, let's see if we can change it up a bit."

Logan called Hughes over. Hughes was to join this group. "I want the Penfolds to have the two of them against you two let's see if you can score against the two of them."Logan refereed the match and he observed that Brooks was not only able to see the pass, he was then able to feed the ball to Hughes to score before the Penfolds could react. The team of Brooks and Hughes were winning by three goals.

After the session Logan caught up with Brooks before he left and asked him if there was any interest in either of his properties. Brooks said, "Sorry still had no interest in either of the properties." Logan said okay and left him to get changed and go home.

That evening Logan went to Mateo's house, he knocked on the door. Mateo's wife opened the door, she was a black lady with long black hair. Logan said, "Good evening, I was wondering if I can see Mateo's I am his coach."

Mateo wife responded with, "I know who you are and Mateo doesn't want to see anyone at the moment."

Logan responded with "Miss, I just want to talk to him." She raised her voice. "Look mister, he doesn't want to speak to you. He said that you betrayed him. He trusted you. My husband is a private man and after the way he was treated by his dad, he has struggled to open up."

139

Logan said "Look Ms. Mateo, I can assure I never told anyone about his act and look, I was happy for him that he was able to follow his passion." Mateo's wife apologised to Logan for her outburst and she took Logan out to their garden where there was a shed, she told Logan he was in there.

Logan knocked on the door of the shed but there was no answer. Logan tried to open the door of the shed but it was also locked. Logan then sat on the ground outside the shed. He then spoke, "Hey Mateo, I just want you to know that it wasn't me and I wouldn't have betrayed you like that. Someone else must have found out and told Tony. Look, I know that you don't believe me, but I just want to say that Tony has left the club and has joined Foxford. If you come back to the team maybe you can show Tony that you are no loser."

There was still nothing, the shed was silent "Logan stood up from the ground and he said, "Look Mateo. Just come to the Cup match against Foxford, even if you don't play, just come and watch the match and then you can come back and hide in your little shed."

Logan walked back into the house and saw Mateo's wife sitting watching the television. Logan said that he got no response from him. Logan asked her where Mateo acquired all the stuff for his Drag outfit. She got up from her chair and found a pen a paper and wrote a number on a piece of paper. She told Logan to give this number a call and they could help him, she asked what he had planned to do.

Logan said, that "Oh I have a couple of surprises for Foxford and Tony."

He then gave a chuckle and said good evening to Mrs Mateo. Logan did say to her as he was leaving saying that Mateo was a lucky man to have a supportive wife like her and she told Logan that she was the lucky one. They both smiled and she gave Logan a hug before he left.

The weekend had come. Logan walked into the pub he sat on the barstool and Lucy came over and said "Haven't seen you in a while, you avoiding me?"

Logan looked up and gave her a smile and said "No, just been busy with the team and stuff."

Lucy then said, "I hear via the grapevine, you clobbered Tony in the face. Not saying he didn't deserve it but in this town, people tend to let Tony get away with a lot of shit as his dad owns most of the town."

Logan laughed and the replied with "The guys, a jerk and I'm glad he is no longer in my team and I don't have to deal with him or his shit anymore." Then Sam walked into the pub, everyone was shocked to see him as he never, ever came in the pub. Sam was dressed in black trousers, with black, shoes a black shirt and his glasses finished his Outfit off. Logan saw him enter, he told Lucy that he will be back in a minute, he had to sort something. Logan walked over to Sam he looked him up and down and then asked "What are you wearing? It looks like you're dressed for a funeral. Well, there's nothing we can do about now. Now, let's grab a seat." They took a table. Logan then said that he was going to the toilet. Logan left the table, but he didn't go to the bathroom, he went and sat back at the bar. Lucy asked him what he was up to, he just told her to "shh" and just watch young love at work.

Then Miranda walked in, she is a white flowery dress she saw Sam and walked over to him and she sat down at the table. Sam got all flustered and went red, he then got off from the table and ran off to the toilet. Lucy said to Logan, "Looks like your master plan has just gone up in smoke."

Logan hit hand on the bar and says, "Oh ye of little faith."

Logan left the bar and went to the washroom to find Sam. Logan saw a pair of black shoes under the cubicle door. He tapped on the door. "Sam" he called, From behind the door he heard Sam's voice. "You lied to. me you said you will help me with Miranda. Yoi know that I can't speak to her, I freeze up. She probably thinks that I am a fool. I should have never trusted you."

Logan said, with "Look buddy, the best way to confront your fears, is to take them head on." Sam then shouted back "I asked for help, I am not ready to go on a date with her." Logan then told Sam "Look Sam, when I spoke to Miranda to ask her if she liked you, she told me that she has been waiting for you to ask her out for years. This is one of the reasons why she spends so much time in the library."

Sam then said "say What did you say?" Logan replied, "Miranda has the hots for you, she likes you the way you are. You don't need my help, you don't need to change. Now stop being a dick and get out there, she is waiting for you." Sam said then "But I can't speak to her, I freeze up and stutter."

"Sam look you just need to forget that she is a young, attractive girl and just treat her as like anyone else."

"But I can't do that." Logan then told Sam "Look, believe it or not I was shy once, but you just need to take a dive off the diving board and jump in."

"But what if I make a fool of myself." he called out as he opened the door. Logan then took him by the right arm and told him, "Sam look, just get out there and talk to the girl. She clearly likes you and you like her, that's all that matters, Now as your coach, I order you now to stop keeping her waiting." Sam gave Logan a hug and then walked out of the washroom and went back to the table where Miranda was sitting.

Then Logan followed him and was going to go and sit back and the bar where Lucy was serving but he noticed Brett doing his normal routine, the beer sitting in front of him. Logan sat down opposite Brett. Brett didn't even acknowledge that Logan had sat in front of him. Until Logan moved the beer from in front of Brett and then speak to him "Hey captain Why so you do buy a beer and then just stare at all evening. There was silence for a few minutes then Brett spoke up. "Look Boss you can captain me on the pitch and order me around but my private life is mine." Logan then reply's with "WO I didn't mean any offence I am just trying to work you out. You work hard in training but in matches it like you are holding back I have seen when you make tackles you never commit to the tackle you will pull out at the last minute but in training you are like a killer and will make great tackle just want to see where I can help."

"Look boss, I know you are trying to help but I don't like to talk."

Logan noticed there was a wedding ring on his finger, so he decided to ask him, "I see that you are married. I haven't seen your wife at any of your matches. Does she not like football?" This question frustrated Brett and he flapped his arms out and knocked the beer off the table. he then screamed, "Oh for fuck's sake, look what you made me do!"

Brett was tried to clear up the mess but started to cry and he uttered the words, "I have messed up so bad I ruined everything." Logan comforted Brett and picked up the empty beer glass and placed onto the table.

Logan asked Brett to tell him everything. Brett told him, "Well, I was a soldier and during my time in service, I saw a lot

143

of stuff that changed me. I lost some good friends who were killed fighting for their country. War is not a place for those of ill disposition. It certainly is not like the movies. Seeing someone being blown up in front of you stays in your memory for ever. Now, when I left the army and I returned home. I struggled with nightmares and wasn't able to find work I started drinking and would be drunk all day and every day. Now this lead me to being angry all the time. I would take my anger out on my wife and one evening, I was very drunk and me and my wife were arguing and screaming at each other and for the first and last time, it was in front of my son and daughter. I let out all my anger out and I hit my wife. I hit her so hard that I knocked her out. The police and paramedics were called and that was the last time my children saw me. I was being handcuffed and taken to the police station. This was over a year ago. My wife didn't press charges and I was released from jail but when I got out. I couldn't bear to go home, so I decided to go as far away from them as possible, so that I couldn't hurt them ever again. I travelled until I got to Dorchester, then saw the pub and I came in for a drink and ordered beer, but just seeing the beer in front of me took me back to what I had done and ever since then no beer shall pass this mouth. I will order a beer and just stare at it to remind me of what I have lost. I also have tried to reign in my anger, so that I don't hurt anyone."

Logan told Brett, "I can't imagine what you witnessed on the battlefield and what you did for your country. Now, I am going to give you a business card for a shrink. It is up to you if you want to call them or not call them. I will tell you that they helped me out, after I had found out about my dad hanging himself. At the time it was hard for me to deal with, but I wouldn't be the man I am today without talking to someone about it. When was the last time you spoke to your wife? Does she even know where you are?"

Brett wiped his eyes, "I haven't spoken to my wife since the day that I hit her. I have been looking for her on the internet, to see how she is doing but no one knows where I am, I just disappeared."

"So your wife is probably still worrying if you're out there alive?" Logan asked.

Brett replied, "It's better that way, I can't hurt her anymore." Brett had enough of the conversation and he got up from the table and fled the pub.

Logan sat back in the chair and put his hands on his head. Lucy walked over with and brings him a beer and a whisky and saidto him, "You look like you need this." Logan looked up at Lucy and he gave her a huge smile as she headed back to the bar.

Chapter 9

Dorchester FC vs Foxford

"Welcome, what a match we have tonight in the fourth round qualifier for the FA cup. The winner earns a place into the first round proper. Neither of these teams have ever made it this far, so there is added incentive. There is already a big rivalry between the teams. We have the Manchester Utd against Liverpool, the Arsenal vs Tottenham or Celtic vs Rangers of the non-league. There is a huge rivalry between both teams and with Tony Sharpe lining up front against his former club.

The local papers have made much about how Tony Sharpe's former team will cope without him now that he has moved to the bigger club.

The bigger story is how Logan, a former Ballon d'Or winner and world cup winner become the coach for Dorkchester. A team that hadn't won a match in over two years until Logan started improving them and now they are on verge of the first round of the FA cup. All they have to do is knockout Foxford.

Well, we will take a short break and we will return with live coverage of Dorkchester vs Foxford."

Mateo arrived at the stadium and he looked around as people looked at him. He felt like he was being laughed at. He rushed through to the changing room, opened the door of the changing room and to his amazement.

When the door swung open Mateo saw his teammates, but they weren't in their normal gear. They had their normal home green shirt on, but instead of football shorts, they woreskirts. the whole team was dressed up they also had wigs. They look like the world's first Drag football team.

Mateo then spoke up, "What is going on here? Why are you all dressed in drag?"

Then Logan dressed in a pink flowery dress with a long blonde wig appeared and said to Mateo, "Mateo, me and the team support you and we decided to show that support to you and that we are not bothered that, for your job, you dress in Drag and sing for people."

Mateo then asked "But what about everyone else, people are going to laugh and take the mick out of us if we go out like that." Logan then patted him on the shoulder and said "Mateo, you are a brave man to get up on stage and to put yourself up there knowing that you will get abuse from some punters. We are going to show the world, okay maybe just the local media, that Drag stars have feelings and need to be respected. There is a true artist behind the glitz and glamour and wigs, The team is behind you. Look, if we can cheer Tank, a man that like to dress in latex and slam other men around a ring, then we will stand by the man who has the best voice of the whole team. Who cares if he wears a dress to do it? Now get changed we've got a match to win and there is someone I know, that we will love to show the team's new look."

"We are minutes away before the teams emerge. Hold on, there seems to be some commotion down in the tunnel. Let's hand over to the pitch side reporter. What is going on Willis?"

"Yes, I am here. There seems to be some shouting between the two teams. Foxford are refusing to come to the field. The referee is trying to sort out was is going on. It appears that Dorkchester FC have come out from the changing room in skirts. The Foxford captain and Tony Sharpe have said that the Dorchester team are making a mockery of them. The referee is trying to find if there is anything in the rules that stops Dorchester FC from coming onto the pitch dressed in drag. Yes, you heard me. The Dorkchester teqm are all dressed as drag. This is in reference to one of the Dorchester players, who is, in his free time, a Drag star."

There was a lot of pushing between the two teams and many raised voices. Tonyis screaming at Logan.

"This is some sort of joke to you, isn't it, do you not have any respect for anyone, just look at you a grown man wearing a dress. Look what you are doing to my team, they are a joke of a team."

Logan answered back with "Tony, last time I checked, you had left the team and now play for Foxford, so correct me if I am wrong, but this is no longer your team."

The Foxford manager, who was dressed in his full tracksuit, came over to Logan and said, Logan "Look, I can fully understand you wanting to support your player after the stuff that was written about him after it came out that he is a cross dresser."

Mateo then spoke up, "Excuse me, I am no cross dresser, I am a Diva star, there's a difference, so check your facts, stud muffin." Mateo turned and flicked his hair into the manager's face. This caused more pushing and shoving between the teams. The Foxford manager was getting in the face of the referee, screamed and shouted at him to sort it out. There was no way his team was taking to the pitch with them dressed like that. There has to be something in the rule. The referee looked in his rulebook, he was also on his phone trying to get some help from his bosses in order to help him make a decision. This carried on for over fifteen minutes. Various players were pushing and shoving. Foxford where shouting homophobic comments at the Dorkchester players. Faggots, Fuck off you Queers, why don't you go to the YMCA, Batty boys.

Tank stayed calm but Brett could see that he was about explode and he knew that if he didn't speak to him. Tank would do something that he would regret. So Brett whispered in his ear, "Save it for the pitch."

The referee then called both the managers to his office and sat them down, he then asked them, "Look, I have consulted my bosses. Now is there anything that can be done, to stop you from going on the pitch dressed like that? This outrage and the backlash and stop it from bringing the came into disrepute. Can we come to a comprise?" Both managers were willing to listen to what the referee came up with.

The referee suggested that the team could walk out onto the pitch in the outfits, walk around the pitch and warm up, then return to the changing room and remove the outfit and return to the pitch in their correct gear. Logan said that he would need to speak to his team to see if they were happy with this before he made decision. The Foxford manager said he would accept this, anything to get the match started. Logan told his team of the suggestion and they were happy with this. So as the team they walked round the pitch. There was lots of boos and cheers. Wolf whistles were heard from the crowd and, from the opposition, there was lots offensive homophobic chants coming from them. Items were thrown at them. But the team stuck together and

149

walked the pitch. The players stuck by their word and got changed into their proper match gear. The only person that didn't change was Logan, he still wore his blue dress. He took his seat on the bench as the team came out. Then the Foxford manager saw that Logan was still wearing a dress. He went back to the referee and screamed in his face again. Logan got up from the bench and walked over and asked, "What's the matter, the team are changed and ready to go. What's up now?" The Foxford manager screamed "Well look at you, you're a man in a dress, you're the manager, you should set example, not dress like that."

Logan replied, "Look, we followed your rule, the team removed what they are wearing." The Foxford manager then shouted at him saying "But look at you're, your still dressed like that!" Logan said,. "Well unfortunately, unlike the players, I haven't got change of outfits and promise you won't tell anyone, but I am naked underneath this outfit. I think that may cause more outrage than me wearing a dress." The Foxford manager, Shouted at Logan, "You think this is funny? Look, I don't know who you think you are, but there is no place for people like that in football." Logan then with his deep voice bellowed back, "Pardon! People like that. What do you mean by that?"

The Manager was taken aback by this and stuttered his words. "You know what I mean, there's no place for them in football it isn't their thing."

Logan then asked him outright, "Let me get this straight, you're saying that football is not for gays."

The manager became more sheepish and then said, "Look, I have nothing against them, I just don't want them in my team."

The manager then realised what he has just said and that the crowd had also heard and now the boos were for him. He heard the words that he was being called homophobic. He tried to return to his bench but before he left Logan said his final words on the matter, "Well unlike you and your team, Dorkchester will gladly accept everyone, no matter who or what they like. Now if you don't mind, I have a match to watch as my team knock you out of the cup, Farewell."

"Well, after a half hour delay, we are getting under way in the cup match ad Dorkchester FC take on their rivals Foxford. Now for those who are just joining us, we have the Dorkchester FC manager who is currently on the bench wearing a blue dress. The Dorkchester team came out dress in drag, but they were persuaded to remove the skirts they were wearing and put on their shorts.

The team say this was done in support of their player Mateo, who is a performer on Drag circuit. After the story broke in the local papers, the club say that there have been a lot of offensive and homophobic comment aimed at the player. I have just received a statement, that has just been passed to me from Logan, the manager of Dorkchester and its says.

Dorchester FC is a club that is open to all. We don't discriminate against anyone, no matter their religion, cultural belief or sexual preference. The club take any acts of abuse, to any of their players, very seriously. The players and I wanted to stand up for our teammate and friend and show that we support him. At Dorkchester, we care more about what players do on the pitch and Mateo is a key part of the team'.

It's clear that Dorkchester fully support and have made a bold statement, in their support of their player. Now some may say 'is this the place to make this statement.'Others will say that this is the perfect time, we have a television camera crew in today, This will get people talking about this issue.

Well the ball is with Tim Penfold, he passes it to his brother Calvin. Thereis a tackle from Harewood, who chips the ball to Robinson, he makes a run to just outside the Dorkchester box, there is a tackle from Champman.

They call Champman the Tank and we can see why he earnt the nickname of the Tank. My sources say that he is not only a part time footballer, he is also an independent wrestler. Yes, he likes to run around dressed in spandex. Well let's hope he doesn't try any wrestling moves on the Foxford team. The ball is back in the centre circle Mateo has the ball, he has just played a pass up to Mcfaden. McFadden is tackled by Daubery. There are lot of niggling tackles in this match, both teams are getting stuck in. There is a lot on the line for them, as it will be the first time that either team have ever played in the FA cup proper.

Brooks now has the ball; he is making a run, another rash tackle has come in from Saunders. There is a lot of pushing and shoving between both teams. The referee is trying to get control of this match.

We are coming up to the forty fourth minute of this match and as yet, neither team have had a single shot on target. There has just been a lot of harsh tackles coming from both teams.

Foxford have a corner, the ball is crossed into the box, Smith punches the ball. Hold on Smith has stayed down on the ground after punching the ball out. There is more pushing and shoving in the box. Let's go to the replay and see what has happened.

Smith punches the ball out he falls to the ground and it appears that Sharpe stamped on Smith's hands. Smith is rolling around in pain, the team doctor is checking Smith's hand.

Unfortunately, we don't have VAR at this ground but if the referee was to have seen this, I'm sure Sharpe would receive a red card. But it was awful challenge, it appears that he stamped on his hand. The referee has booked Sharpe. It appears that Smith is staying on, but he does seem to have a bit of discomfort in his hand. Well, the referee has blown the whistle for the end of the first half. We are still at nil nil and neither team have tested either keeper. The biggest talking point of the first half, is the stamping on Smith by Sharpe. Well let's hope that we see some more shots in this match we will return after the break."

The team were in the changing room after the first half battle The doctor was checking over Harvey and his hand over. Logan walked over to them and asked them how bad the damage was. The doctor said "it isn't good, I suspect that he may have broken a bone. Weare going to have to take to him to hospital for an X ray." Logan then said "Okay I will take him off and get him to hospital." Then Harvey piped up, "No No. Look, I want to get them back. Look, I am not going, Look, put me up front and Escobar in goal. I have something to show Tony." The doctor advised that he fills that he needed to go to the hospital and get his hand X rayed." Harvey said he would make the doc a deal, he will finish the match and then he will promise he would go to the hospital. He told the doc to strap his hand up.

Logan and the Doc spoke and under duress he strapped Smith's hand up and the team got ready for the second half.

"Well, welcome back. Let's hope the second half livens up and we get some shots on goal. We have one change but it seems a strange one, Escobar and has gone in goal, yet Smith the keeper has moved up front. This seem another bizarre tactic by Logan, the Dorkchester manager. Who is still wearing a dress. Well, let's get back to the action. The ball is with is with Angelos, who passes it onto Rodgers, who plays it along to Smith. Smith turns from the defender, Smith hit the shot, it on its way into the top corner. The keeper just manages to get a hand to the ball and tips it over the goal.

Wow, why has smith has been hiding in goal when he can hit the ball like that. The corner is put in oh my, Smith on the volley and has just hit the ball into the back of the net. Dorkchester are now one nil up. Their goalkeeper Smith, who moved up front, has just put them into the lead.

Escobar hits the ball up field and Smith has the ball again, he has twisted past the first defender, he has just gone straight through two more, he is one on one with the keeper and he slots it home for the second. Well, it looks like Logan has just unleashed there secret weapon on Foxford and it is their keeper Smith.

Sharpe has the ball for Foxford, he is trying to take on the Dorkchester defenders by himself. Harewood is in space, all Sharpe has to do is pass to him, but he is trying to go it alone. He has just gone crashing into Champman or the Tank. The ball has fallen to Elliot, who launches the ball up the pitch, Angelos has chipped the ball into the path of Smith and at the volley he launches another shot on goal and would you believe it Dorkchester are now three nil up.

The referee has blown the final whistle and Dorkchester are on their way to the first-round draw of the FA cup. This team has pulled off a surprise here. Let's go down to pitch and get comments from Logan the manager of Dorkchester.

"Yes, I am here with Logan the manager of Dorkchester FC First of all, before we get to you, and why the team came out in drag, you are in the First round FA cup."

Logan responded to the reporter, "Yes, the team are so excited about being in the FA cup, we are looking forward to challenging ourselves against a league team for the first time in the club history. This is a big moment, not only for the team but the town as well."

"Let's get into why you chose to wear this dress."

But before Logan could answer this question Tony came over and started pushing Logan and berating him "What the hell was that? You should be ashamed yourself. What do you look like? There is no place for people like you in the game. I don't want them at my club. The fucking gays or faggots in my team they should play in their own league."

This was all being recorded on the television. Logan then responded with, "Pardon, can you say that again? Look, unlike you, my team are open to all. This club will support and accept everyone, no matter if they are straight, gay, bi or trans. It doesn't matter, they are all the same to me. I think you are just annoyed that we beat you fairly and with a drag star in the team."

This angered Tony who pushed Logan. Logan was caught off guard and fell to the floor. The stewards and referee got in between them and Tony was escorted away.

"We would like to apologise to anyone who was offended by any of the comments. We don't condone any homophobic views on this programme."

The team were at the pub celebrating their win, waiting for the draw for the FA cup first round. Logan sat at the bar, Lucy came over to him and she said it was brave of him to stand by Mateo. Logan told her that he would do it again in a heartbeat. Logan said that he loved everyone and respected all sexes and everyone should be able to express themselves. Lucy gave him a peck on the cheek. Logan asked what that was for but before she could answer, the Foxford team who was being led by Tony came in the pub. Tony walked over to Logan and got in his face and screamed at him, "I told you to stay away from my girl and you made me look stupid on television, and making out that I hate gays."

Logan interrupted with, "Firstly, I think you will find you made yourself look stupid. You didn't need my help with that and secondly, she is not your girl."

Tony was very angry with this. He clenched his fists and he went to hit Logan in the face, but just as he did, Tank stepped in the way and Tony's fist hit Tank in the face. Tank did not flinch but Tony was holding his hand and because he was in pain. Then another player from the Foxford team launched a bottle and and hit the Tank in the head. Then, the next thing the two teams are pushing and shoving and punches were thrown. The pub was now a battle between the teams. Glasses were thrown. Tank picked up one of the Foxford players and slammed him through a table, smashing it to pieces. The Penfolds twins were a tag team against another player. Brett knocked out two of the Foxford players. The police soon arrived and were splitting and separating the players from each other. Logan manage to sneak out from all the commotion Lucy waved to him and he followed her up to her room above the pub. She told him to grab a seat and she gave him a drink, then thanked him for sticking up for her.

Then she said "Do you know, the first time I met you I thought that you were nothing but another sleazy jerk. But seeing how you have been helping the team and their families, I think there is a good side to you. You have grown on me."

Logan laughed and gave her smile. He then asked, What did you ever see in Tony, he's just another shmuck.

"He belittles people and thinks he's better than everyone else."

Lucy said "I fell for his looks that's all it was, but realised looks weren't everything and also, him, cheating on me caused us to break up. When I was going out with him, I got close to his mum and I became friends with her and this is why I kept in contact with him and stayed friends. He does make me laugh and he can be a real gentleman."

Lucy put some music on and said that she was going to see what is happening downstairs and she would be back. Lucy went down to the pub and came back a few minutes later. She looked at Logan and said, "The pub is wrecked. I am going to have to spend the rest of the night cleaning up. There are smashed glasses and broken tables all over the pub. It looks like a riot kicked off but it is safe for you to go now and thank you again for sticking up for me."

Logan looked up at her and said, "It is okay, I will help you clear up, it is partly my fault that the pub got ruined."

Logan pulled himself up from the chair and followed her back down to the bar area. Logan helped Lucy clean up the bar and clear the smashed table. Lucy filled a bin bag with rubbish. Logan and Lucy both reached for a bottle but their hands touched. Lucy flinched when she realised that her hand was in his. "Oh, I'm so sorry." Logan told her that it was okay. He then told her "Why, you have such nice soft hands."

Lucy squirmed when he made that remark. He followed it with, "Why are you still working in this bar? You are a very attractive young woman. Why are you wasting your life in this bar now my uncle has left. When I sell the pub. I could help you settle somewhere else. Get you setup somewhere nice."

Lucy looked Logan straight in the face and said, "This is my home. I love this pub. This pub saved my life. I would be in a very different place, if it wasn't for your uncle and this pub. Yes, I have had some bad memories but there has been some great memories. I really hope who ever takes on this place will be willing to keep me on. I don't know what I would do without this place."

Logan smiled at her and said, "I will promise I will make sure any deal for the pub includes you as part of it."

Their eyes met and Lucy and Logan just stare at each other. It was as if time had been paused. They just gazed at each other. Lucy went in for a kiss but for some reason Logan pulled away and he gets up. Lucy looks puzzled as to why he wouldn't kiss her. Then Logan stuttered his words, "Lu lug Lucy, would you like to go for a date with me?"

Lucy seemed puzzled by this but she gladly accepted his offer of a date. They made arrangements to meet on Saturday. They finished clearing up the bar before Logan said goodnight. He kissed Lucy on her cheek and said good night before he left. Lucy rubbed her face after the kiss and gave him a huge smile.

Chapter 10

The First Round of the Cup

Logan was awoken by his phone ringing. "Hello," he said. On the other end of the line was Brooks. He said that they had an offer for both the pub and the cottage but he wasn't going to like who had put in the offer. Logan asked who it was and he was told that it was Mr Sharpe and he had put a decent offer for them. Logan then said there was no way that he would sell to the Sharpe, no matter what. So he can tell them to shove their offer so far up there arse, that it is never seen again. Logan fell back to sleep. Then an hour later there is a knock at his door. He dragged himself from the bed and opened the door. It was Harvey, he looked scared. Logan asked "What's the matter?" Harvey said "The Dorkchester board have called a meeting and they have asked me to bring you. It appears that they were not too happy with our antics in the match and the bar brawl." Logan nodded and got himself dressed and they headed to the club.

Logan and Harvey walked into the meeting room. Where there was Mr Sharpe, Harvey's dad and there was the Doctor, who not only is the town and club doctor but also, a member of the board. There was a lonely chair in the middle of the room Logan took the hint and sat down in the middle of the room. Harvey's dad started speaking, "Logan, we have called you here today due to the impact your act had on the club, the club have been made to look like a joke. Your antics have brought shame to the club. Now we understand that you have improved the team and morale of the whole town has gone up. But we draw the line of having members of our club walking around in a dress." Logan then bit back with, "Look, I stand by my actions. I have been working with these players, they have welcomed me into their town and into their lives and have shown me great respect and when I see that one of those players is being abused and some of the stuff that was said to him was very offensive and hurtful, I had to show him that we stand by him and stand together, no matter what."

Then Mr Sharpe slammed his hand on the table and shouted, "You have embarrassed and brought shame to this club and then there the little act of the bar fight. Logan, why don't you just take my offer for your crappy pub and your uncle's dive of a cottage and leave us alone. The town no longer wants you here." Then all of a sudden, the rest of the Dorkchester team came storming in the room. Harvey's dad shouted, "This is a closed meeting, you cannot be here." Tim Penfold stepped forward and said

"We are here to stand by our manager. If you sack him then you will have to sack all of us." Harvey's dad said, "Son, have a word with your team."

Harvey then looked at his dad and told him, "Sorry dad but the answer is no and also, I just want to say that I am no goalkeeper, I am going to be this club's best striker and score more goals than I would ever save." Then McFadden walked forward and told them, "Logan is going to help so that my son will be able to come and see me play, so he gets my support."

Then next up was Mateo. In his diva voice he says "Logan is more of man than any of you gentleman."

Rodgers was up next "I spent my career following Tony around but Logan has taught me to be my own man and I am a much better player."

Brooks then came up and laid a piece of paper on the table that said 'no deal'. Then Penfold's brother came forward and said that Logan taught them to work together. Then Sam, who was wearing his mask, and stood in front of his dad and he then removed his mask. The doctor stood up and screamed at his son "What are you doing? You're not a member of this team." Sam then looked his dad straight in the eyes and said,

"Dad, I am a footballer and I am not going to be studying as a doctor."

The doctor, stood and he was hitting his hand on table, he then screamed back. "What? You will be on going to study to be a doctor!"

Sam got closer to the table and said, "No I won't be, medicine isn't for me. I failed my exams. I am good at football and Logan say's I have huge potential and with the correct training will do well."

The doctor said, "Oh no you won't, no son of mine is going to waste their time kicking a ball around."

Then the rest of the team all stepped forward and all at the same time said, "Pardon, Sam is one of us. It you don't like it, tough."

Then Harvey's dad said, "Look, this not getting us anywhere. I think it is in the club's best interests if we agree that Logan can continue in his role at the club for now. As long as he promises no more antics like what happened against Foxford". Logan stood up and said, "I promise that I won't do anything like this in the future and will focus in helping the team to reach it's full potential."

The three board members looked at each other and nodded. Mr Sharpe, the Doctor and Harvey's dad started talking between themselves. Mr Sharpe not look too pleased about it, but realised that they wouldn't have a club if all the team left, they had to save face.

But just as it looked like it was all over, Mr Glass walked up to them but Harvey's dad said, "Look, we already agreed to not to sack Logan. This matter is closed." But Mr Glass smiled and said, "I am gay and proud to be." He then turned and walked out of the room. The room went silent.

The next day, at training the team were all getting ready to go onto the training pitch? Mr Glass stood in the doorway, he looked at all the players and he spoke to them. "Yes, I am gay and seeing how you all stood behind Mateo, has given me the strength to come out. I have also, as of last night, I have proposed to my partner and we plan on getting married. I would like to invite you all to my special day. I hope that now I have come out to you, that you don't treat me any differently and you show me the same respect that you always have."

The room all looked at him and then, one by one, came over and congratulated him. They all Agreed that it would be an honour to be there and they wouldn't miss it. Well, apart from Rodger, who said that as long as there wasn't any footy on, then he would be there. Logan was the last one to go up to him he said it was very brave of him to come out to his teammates and he was honoured to have given him the bravery to speak up.

Mr Glass told Logan. "Yes, not even my mum and dad know that I am gay: When I moved here and started working, I met Ben and we hit of and after a few months of dating, we moved into together. My Dad thinks that Ben is just my housemate and has no clue that we sleep in the same bed. Once I decided I had the strength to come out to my teammates and seeing how they reacted, then hopefully it will give me the push to finally tell my parents the truth. I have invited my parents to the FA Cup first round against Torquay United, then me and Ben will take them out for a meal after and tell them."

Logan gave Mr Glass a hug he then said "Your parents should be proud of everything you have accomplished and will be even more prouder of you when we knock Torquay out of the cup." Both laughed and then they headed out to the training field to do some drills.

It was the evening of Logan and Lucy's date. Lucy had arranged cover for the pub. Logan had dressed in black trousers with black shoes. He also wore a yellow shirt with a collar. He was meeting Lucy at the pub, he had organised for a limo to take them out into the city for a show and meal. Logan went across to the pub he went in the pub the whole place went quiet. The barman was behind the bar, he shouted to him. "she is getting dressed.She said to go on up." Logan went up to the apartment, knocked on the door but there was no answer. He pushed the door open and walked in.

He couldn't see Lucy around, so he called out for her. He heard her saying to take a seat and she would be with him shortly.

After a few minutes Lucy walked into the room. Logan stood up from the chair that he was sitting in. As Logan looked at Lucy and he saw that she was wearing the same dress that he wore for the cup match. Logan then said "Well, I have to say, it looks a lot better on you, than it did on me." Lucy laughed and said, "I thought you might like this one." She grabbed a blue purse that matched her dress and they headed down to bar area. They entered the pub to a lot of wolf whistles and cheering.

As Lucy left the pub, she saw the long black Limousine. She gasped and then said, "Wow I have never been in a limo before,

Even when I was with Sharpe, he never treated me like this."

Logan opened the limo's door and Lucy stepped in. A bottle of champagne and two glasses awaited them. Lucy sat took a in the limo and Logan sat next to her. He then took the bottle of champagne and poured them each a glass. Lucy took a sip of the champagne she giggled and said "The bubbles always go straight to my head."

Logan then told the the driver that they were ready and the limo pulled away. They looked out of the window and saw that everyone in the pub had come out and were watching and waving as the limo drove off. It was a forty-five drive into the city. Lucy said "So, Mr big shot football star, tell me about the real you, the man behind the football, There's a different side to you, one that the papers and the TV doesn't show. I have seen how you have helped all Dorkchester FC players, not only off the pitch but on it. You are a truly good man." Logan looked into Lucy's beautiful eyes it was like gazing into space, he could look at them forever.

"I have had a lot of up and downs in my life and things have not always gone to plan for me and after my dad took his own life, I was kind of on my own for a while and my football started to suffer. Then I met Zimmerman. He helped me and saved me. He was the first guy that helped me and I saw the love and respect that he gave his daughter and even if he didn't agree with her life choices. On his death bed, he made promise something, although I did break one of the promises and have only just pulled myself around. The two things he told me to do is not go back to my old ways and to help people in need. He said that if you help them, they will help you back and it was only when I was on the coach ride up to Dorkchester, when talking to a nice old lady, that I kind of remember what I had promised. After my football career was cut short, I kind of went off the rails, so to speak, and wasn't in a good place I pushed my friends away. Coming to Dorkchester has actually helped me and given me a purpose and I am starting to like it here."

Lucy then asked Logan, "Does that mean you will not be selling up and may stick around for longer."

Logan quickly responded with, "I don't know about that. I'm still unsure about returning to the city but I have to say, with views like this, I may be persuaded to stick around, who knows." He looked Lucy up and down admiring her legs then blurted out, "I can so see why you got the nickname 'legs' They are like a work of art, just so naturally beautiful."

Lucy squirmed at this compliment and started to blush. She then said to him. "Well, you are such a charmer, no wonder you have the reputation you have with women."

Logan told her, "Well, don't always believe what you read. Not all of it is true."

The driver then from the front of the limo said, "We have arrived at the playhouse." Logan got out of the limo first, then he held the door open for Lucy as she slid out of the limo. She then looked up and saw the grand theatre. It was on old building, with banners advertising the Ballet. She noticed that there was a red carpet. Sh then looked at Logan, and in awe, said, "Wow.

It's like I am walking up the red carpetfor a world premiere."

Logan took Lucy's hand and walked with her up to the grand door of the theatre where the usher was standing. Logan showed the tickets and the usher showed them to where their seats were. They were in a private box. There was wine in an ice bucket, with two glasses in between two chairs and there was also a pair of binoculars.

Lucy saidto Logan, "I have only seen things like this in movies, I never thought I would experience being in a private box." She then sat in the big red chair and picked up the binoculars, She looked at the theatre and the details ofthe building. She looked at the stage and she could see the dark red curtains.Once they sat down,Logan then passed her a glass of wine. The music began and the curtains started to pull open. As they opened there was one ballet dancer stood in the middle of the stage. Shewas dressed in a full white ballet costume. They were able to see the dancer's face and blonde hair. Lucy took the binoculars and watched as the dancer started to move around the stage. She was as if she was flying across the stage. Then the tone of the music got louder and faster. Suddenly male ballet dancer appeared on the stage, He was dressed in a full red costume. The two dancers danced entwined, it was as if they were moving as one. Another male dancer appeared on stage, dressed in a white costume. The new dancer pulled the girl from the man in red and she danced off the stage Then two male dancers danced together. It looked Then the man in white and the man in red dance but it was as if they were battling and fighting. Lucy then turned to Logan, looked him in the eye and she asked him, "Do you understand what's happening?"

Logan laughed and said, "No clue I chose the ballet as I thought it was something you would like."

Lucy nibbled her top lip and said, "Not to bother about the Ballet but the company is starting to grow on me."

The first half of the ballet finished and Lucy went off to washroom. When she returned there was another bottle of wine and Lucy's glass was full again. Lucy looked at Logan and said, "Are you trying to get me drunk?" Lucy took a sip of her wine

166

and sat back in the chair for the second half of the ballet. Lucy then picked up the binoculars but rather than looking at the stage, she turned to look at Logan. She started at his black shoes and slowly moved up his leg looking at him moving the binoculars following up his body she then hovered over his groin area. Logan asked how she was finding the second half of the ballet. Her response was: "I am really enjoying the view I really like the perks of the binoculars." Logan stood up and began to walk across to Lucy. Lucy still had the binoculars and watched watching him move closer and closer to her. Logan is then stood directly in front of her why she held the Binoculars his eyes where at the end of them. He moved the binoculars from her eyes and he moved his lips to hers and kissed her on lips. He could taste the cherry of her lipstick. He then looked in the eyes and said,. "Hmm, cherry lipstick. Why look, when you can touch."

Lucy started to swoon, she then leant forward and then kissed Logan. This time, their lips were connected for longer. As they kissed, their eyes were also locked together. They were distracted and pulled away from each other lips when they heard the applause. They turned to look at the stage, the ballet had finished. Logan and Lucy started to applaud. Then they both laughed and smiled at each other. Logan took Lucy's hand and they left the theatre. He then ushered her into the limo that was waiting and the driver then took them to a five star restaurant.

As Logan took her for the final part of their date, They got out of the limo and Logan took Lucy's by the hand and he walked with her into the restaurant. The waiter is said to Logan, Ah Mr Logan, we have your table ready." They were taken to a table for two. There was a glass vase holding the most beautiful flowers. Lucy had to smell them, she put her nose into flower head and she said, "They smell as amazing as they look. The waiter then pulled out Lucy's chair and she took her seat. The waiter laid her a blue napkin in her lap. She watched as the waiter did the same to Logan. Once they are both seated, the waiter passed them each a menu. Lucy looked at the menu and she gasped and blurted out, "Holy shit, how much?"

Logan could see Lucy was taken aback by the menu. He then asked her "Is everything okay?"

Lucy smiled at him and told him. "Yes, I am just not used to going to these fancy places. The nicest place I have ever eaten out was McDonalds. I'm not used to the prizeof these meals. They probably cost more than I would spend on month's worth of food."

Logan said to her, "Lucy, you are a truly amazing woman and deserve to be treated like the star you are."

Lucy was embarrassed and started to blush, She sat back in the chair as she looked up, she saw the golden chandelier hanging from the ceiling. Lucy called out, "Holy fuck."

Logan laughed and smiled at Lucy. The waiter returned and ask if they were ready to order. Lucy was unsure of what to have, as she didn't know what half of it was. She asked Logan to order for her, Logan smiled at her, then he turned to the waiter and said, "We will have my usual.". The waiter said, "Of course Mr Logan." Logan then ordered a bottle of the house wine to go with the meal.

Lucy asked Logan what he had ordered. He looked at her and said, "Oh,you will see you won't be disappointed." Fifteen minutes later, the waiter returned with the meal. He put the first meal in front of Lucy. To her surprise, what was laid in front of her, was not what she expected to see in a five star restaurant. What was presented was a tower of burgers. There was a bun, on top of which was a burger, red lettuce and tomatoes. Then there another burger and after that was melted cheese. There was then a seeded bun topping

tower burger. There was a flag

holding it all together. Also on the plate was a portion of onion rings, with curly fries a side of garden peas. Logan had the same the waiter returned with a glass bowl and he placed this in the middle of the table. Lucy looked into the bowl and saw that there was a bottle of Ketchup that was with surrounded byice. Lucy then said to Logan, "Wow, this is biggest Burger I have ever seen, I don't remember seeing this on the menu."

Logan replied, with "Shh, it isn't on the menu, but I am friends with the head chef, so he makes it for me. Don't tell anyone else as I am the only one who allowed to have ketchup in here." Lucy gave him a smile and laughed. She leant forward and picked up the ketchup and tapped it onto her plate, she then passed it to Logan.

They enjoyed the meal and laughed and joked together, There was a very good atmosphere and a real spark between them, they couldn't stop looking at each other. The evening continued and after they had finished the first course Lucy said she was too full to have any pudding. Logan paid his bill then he stood and pulled Lucy's chair out and helped from her chair. Lucy was a little unsteady on her feet, probably due to the champagne and the wine she had. She needed Logan to help her stand and they walked out to the awaiting Limo. It was probably to the fresh air that allowed the alcohol to kick in as Lucy needed Logan to pretty much pick her up and put her into the limo. Whilst she slurred her words, she flirted with Logan and said, "I spank mo. mery munch bor a mery bood might you have gotten me drunk is mis so you can bet into my knickers mot that I am complaining I noanna see vant you mare packing." She leant in to kiss him but

169

just as she did, the limo started to move. Lucy lost her balance and fell into Logan's lap. Lucy rested her head on Logan's lap and looked at him. Logan ran his hand through her hair and gazed at her. Their eyes again locked together and Logan watched as Lucy slowly drifted off to sleep in the limo, her head resting on his lap. They arrived back at the pub from the city. Lucy had slept all the way back. Logan gently tapped her on top of her head to wake her up. She bolted upright, with a fright and at first was unsure where she was. Then the limo driver opened the door. Lucy stepped out followed by Logan. They walked up to the pub and Lucy pulled out her key from her purse and opened the door. She looked at Logan and whilst still slurring her words said, "I have had a great evening, mould mike to come in for a night cap." She stepped inside and Logan followed Lucy through the door, without saying a word, he pushed the door closed behind them.

Logan turned and kissed Lucy on her cherry lips, locking their mouths together and embraced. Logan noticed the pool table, and whilst he kissed Lucy, slowly moved her towards the pool table. He then lifted her and rested her bottom on the edge of the table, He slid the dress off her shoulders and so that the dress dropped to the floor. Logan looked at Lucy as she sat in front of him, in her blue knickers and bra. Logan moved his hands and unclipped her blue bra and slips this of her shoulders and her bra dropped to the floor. Logan stared at Lucy she was now in front of him wearing just her blue knickers, which were slightly see through. Logan looked at Lucy breasts, they were perfect and plump and just the perfect, natural size.

Logan stood for a few minutes admiring them but suddenly looked away and said, "I can't do this, it feels different. I am sorry I have to go."

Logan kissed Lucy on her cheek and he then turned and

made a hasty retreat out of the pub. Leaving Lucy sat on the pool table, gobsmacked not quite understanding what had just happened. She sat for a few moments and hoped that he would come back, but he didn't.

Lucy jumped off the pool table, she lent down and picked up her dress and bra from the floor. She and locked the door of the pub and then went upstairs to her bed, still puzzled as to what just happened. She said to herself, "Does he not find me attractive? Am I ugly? What did I do wrong? Is there something wrong with my body? Am I too fat for him?" Lucy threw herself into her bed and started to cry.

Over the next couple of weeks Logan avoided Lucy. The team had a few league matches in the build up to the next cup match. They had managed two draws and two losses and they are still bottom of the league table. Luckily for them, they were at the bottom of the football pyramid, so they couldn't go any lower.

It was the day of the first-round match against Torquay. The team arrived at the ground, they were excited about playing in the biggest match in the club's history.

"Welcome to Torquay United against Dorkchester FC, the first round of the FA cup. The teams are coming out onto the pitch. I can confirm that there are no men in dresses on the pitch and Logan is dressed in a track suit. I have seen that there are a few fans in the crowd wearing dresses. It looks like there is a stag do. In the Torquay end I can see one of them wearing a sash, that says Groom to be. The interesting part of the team news is that Smith, the Dorkchester goalie, after his exploits in the match against Foxford, he is now no longer in goal, he is leading the strike force. Well, let's get on with the match.

The game has kicked off and Brooks has the ball he passes

it to McFadden, who has a shot at goal, it has gone wide. Torquay kick the ball up field and there is a scramble in the middle of the field. Rodgers has come away with the ball. He launches it across the penalty box, McFadden just misses out on connecting with the ball, it far in the opening twenty minutes of the match. It looks like Dorkchester have the better of the match, it looks like they are most likely to be opening the scoring. Just as I say that Torquay had a shot on goal and just missing the goal Escobar was scrambling for the ball. We are reaching the thirty third minute and we are still locked at nil. The Penfold twins are playing the ball between each other and they put a cross into the box, Smith collects the ball he then turns and hits a shot on the goal and it hits the back of the net. Dorkchester are one nil up in the thirty sixth minute of the match. Is this FA cup fairy tale going to continue for the tiny team of Dorkchester. The referee brings the first half to an end. How is the Torquay manager going to sort out his team and what can they do in the second half."

Logan brought his team drink and whilst they are all grabbing their juices, Logan stood on a table and shouted out "Okay team. We are halfway into the next round. We need to make sure we defend as team we need to make sure we are chasing every ball. We need to attack as a team, we need to see this through. I want to see Dorchester FC into the second round of the cup." The team all cheered together as they headed out for the second half.

"Torquay have made two subs, they have brought on two attacking players to help get back on level terms. Torquay have the ball they are pushing forward. They play the ball across the box, but it is cleared and launched up field. Torquay attack again with the ball but they are crowded out and can't get the ball away.

172

Torquay just can't seem to break down the defence. Every time they get the ball, eight they have Dorkchester players surrounding them and they just can't do anything with the ball. Again, Torquay tries to get the ball forward but the ball is behind for a corner for Torquay. Now the corner is slingshot in and Escobar plucks the ball out from mid-air. He throws the ball out to Wise, who is just running with the ball. He is running the length of the pitch, he is now just past the centre circle. He is still going, he gets past the last defender and now he is one on one with the keeper and he slides the ball past the keeper and now Dorkchester are now two nil up. Have they booked themselves into the second round? Who would have thought that team will be capable of another upset? But here we are. Torquay kick off and they now have to throw everything at Dorkchester now but with the way Dorkchester have been playing, I can't see them doing it in the last minutes of the match."

The referee called the final whistle and all the Dorkchester players jumped around on the pitch and hugged each other. Logan joined his players in celebrating their win in the cup.

The team were all getting ready to go to the pub to celebrate the win. Logan sat on the bench and held his head in his hands, none of the other players noticed apart from McFadden, who stopped and asked "You okay boss? Anyone would think we had just lost the match." Logan lifted his head from his hand and said to, him "Can I be frank with you?"

McFadden said, of "Of course, what is troubling you?"

Logan then sat up more on the bench and looked at him and said, "Well, I took Lucy out for a date and end of the evening I failed to deliver."

McFadden spoke up. "Lots of men your age go through this,

173

you can buy the special blue pill, it is nothing to be ashamed of boss,"

Logan very angrily responded with, "What! No, there is anything wrong with that. I am very able to satisfy a woman, I have never had any complaints. It is something very different when I was with her. When I was looking at her sweet sexy naked body, I felt I wanted more than just fucking her. What is wrong with me?"

McFadden looked at him, laughed and told him, "BOSS! I think that you're in love and by the looks of it, for the first time. In your past, you probably just shagged them and then moved on, but with Lucy I think that you want more and don't want to ruin it. So, there is nothing wrong with you. Now my advice is to you is tell her how you feel and do it fast before it's too late because a girl that fine, won't wait forever,"

Logan shook his head and said, "Love! Don't be daft. The only woman that I have ever loved was my mum. It was more like she wasn't my type I will have to find some other girl at the pub tonight and see if it is just a blip."

McFadden laughed out loud and said, "If you say so boss, but believe me, when you do find love, you need to make sure you jump on, it as love does not come around every day. When I met my wife, I knew straight away she would be mine forever."

Logan then got up and as he walked past, he said one final thing. "Forever seems a long time to be with one person. Sorry that isn't for me. Now let's go and join the rest of the team to celebrate the win."

Chapter 11

The Second Round of the Cup

Logan met the team at the pub they were already on the beers Logan was handed a beer and he joined the team in their celebrations. Logan saw Lucy was busy at the bar. He gave her glance, but she didn't acknowledge him. Logan noticed there was a group of girls at a table drinking and Logan walked over to their table, laughing and saw there was an empty chair. There were three girls and Logan sat with them, He said, "Hi." to He asked what they wanted to drink, all three of them asked for Bacardi and coke. Logan gave them and smile and walked over to the bar. Logan waited till Lucy had finished serving a customer and he then waved her over. Lucy moved down the bar to him and looked at him in and said, "It look like you have made some friends, what do you want for your bimbos, sorry the ladies you're with."

Logan just responded with, "Can I get three Bacardi and cokes?" Lucy moved away and come back with the drinks he had asked for. She slammed them down on the counter and then moved onto the next customer. She watched him out of the corner of her eye as he walked back over to the girls and handed them their drinks.

Lucy kept an eye on them all evening. She watched Logan flirting with the girls, it seemed like he had taken a liking to the tall, red head with glasses, she noticed that his hand was resting

175

on her thigh. As the evening drew to close Lucy noticed Logan whispering into the girl's ear. They then got up, but Lucy was distracted by a couple of lads who were having an argument. They pushed each other and a Lucy had to sort them out and wasn't able to see what happened to Logan and the girl.

Logan and the tall girl with glasses, had left the pub together and got into a taxi and they went to Logan's house. Logan and the girl kissed as they walked to the front door. As Logan opened the door, they fell through the doorway. Logan caught the girl before she fell to the floor. Hepulled her into his arms and they kissed again. Logan pulled her into the bedroom and pushed her onto the bed. He knelt down and took off of her heels and started to run his hands up her legs. He moved his hands up her skirt and after a few seconds, he pulled down her underwear. He threw this to the floor. Then he moved his hand and started to put his finger inside her vagina and started to move it around. He could see her starting to squirm.

He then pulled off her skirt and Logan stood up and looked at her. She still had her top but she wore nothing below the waist. This was a woman who took pride in her vagina. There was a tidy, trimmed patchof hair just above it. Logan took off his belt and then pulled down his trousers. He then removed the shirt that he was wearing, this was the moment when the girl also removed her top and bra. She laid back, naked back in the bed. Logan pulled out a condom from his drawer, opened it up and put in on. He got on top of her and slid his cock inside her. They started fucking and Logan pounded away on her and they both had hot and passionate sex together.

The next day Logan woke up, he turned and saw the girl in the bed next to him. She still wore her glasses. Logan got up and went to the toilet and the girl started to stir. As he came back from the toilet he noticed that the girl was already getting dressed. She walked over to him and kissed him on the cheek and then said, "Mary said you will be a good fuck I'll see you around." She then walked out of the bedroom, leaving Logan stunned. Later Logan that day got a call later the day saying that the draw for the second round of the cup has taken place and they had been drawn at home to Stevenage. They were one match away from possibly playing a premier league club. Dorkchest, the club that hadn't even had a premier league team play them in a friendly. What a prospect that would be.

It was two weeks after the cup match and Dorkchester had lost all their league games. They were still bottom of their league. Logan had a call, on his phone when he answers it was Mr Glass. He seemed panicked and said, "Terry is missing. He didn't turn up at school today and he hasn't been home. His mum is worried, she told me that after he had argument with his stepdad, he stormed off. He has asked the rest of the team and asked if anyone else has seen him but nobody has any clue where he is." He asked if Logan had any idea where he could be. Logan said he didn't but he would come and help find him. Logan added that he had an idea where he could be.

Logan got a taxi to the Dorkchester stadium, he went to the pitch and just as he thought, there he was. Sitting in the middle of the pitch. Logan approached him, Terry looked up and saw Logan walking over to him. He said to Logan, "Leave me alone, I just want to be left alone."

Logan carried walking over and sat beside him and began to talking to him. "So, what's up?"

Terry didn't acknowledge him and pretended to ignore him, so Logan carried on talking "There are a lot of people worried about you and wondering where you are."

This set him off and he angrily turned to Logan and screamed, "No one cares about me, if they did, they wouldn't be marrying that prick, he will not replace my dad. Why does she want to marry him anyway? What does he offer?"

Logan replied, with "Look, I don't know what happened with your family, but I can tell you from experience that when I lost my mum, my life was never the same again. My dad was never really there for me, all he wanted was the money I was bringing home. This new guy in your mum's life will never replace your dad and your dad is one of the good ones unlike mine. I did not have a lot of love in my family. Your mum is worried about you, she does care, surely you don't want to worry her and just want to see she is happy."

Terry then said "Yes, I want my mum to be happy and don't want her to worry, but why did it have to be him?" Logan stands up and then held a hand out. Terry took his hand and stood up. They walked of the pitch together and Logan took Terry home to his mum, who had been crying. When she saw Terry neither said anything She just ran to him and hugged him. Terry's mum boyfriend came and tapped Logan on the shoulder and said, "Thank you for finding him. His mum has been worrying. She's been beside herself. He didn't take the news of our engagement well."

Logan turned to him and said "He's just scared that you are going to replace his dad." The bloke then said "Yes, his dad was my best friend and his death affected the town and after his death, me and Sylvia grieved together. We became close and this is when we started to build our relationship, Terry found it hard, as he saw me as like uncle and now I am dating his mum. It was a big adjustment. But I truly love his mum and just want her to be happy with me."

Logan then tapped the guy on the shoulder and said "I think you all need to talk about your worries and maybe get some therapy. I can give you a number of a few therapists that have helped me sort out my problems. This may help with your issues. I know when I lost my mum, it had a big impact on my family."

Logan wiped a tear away from his eye before he said goodbye to the family and left.

During the next few weeks, in the build up to the next cup match they had lost all their league matches and were still rock bottom. The pundits and bookies predicted that Stevenage were favourites and Dorkchester had no real hope of coming up with another win therefore didn't have a chance of appearing against the big boys in the third round of their cup.

"Good afternoon, we are at Dorkchester, the team that surprised us in the cup match against Torquay United. Dorkchester are the team that have been in the headlines, not just for their action on the pitch, but their actions off it. You'll remember that the team came out dressed in drag, in support of their teammate who is a professional drag artist."

"Well, the team are coming out on the pitch. What can we expect this time around? Dorchester, the lowest team of the non-league they are bottom of the bottom, but will we have a huge surprise in the cup? We are under way and Hughes, who is no longer wearing a face mask, is on the ball. He flicks it a across and Glass, who spins two defenders picks it up and has a low shot on goal and it is in the goal. What a start for Dorkchester. in a matter of minutes they have gone one nil up. Stevenage must have been sleeping Glass, who is a Head teacher has just given the Stevenage defenders a masterclass and now it looks like

Dorkchester could do it again. The ball is up in the air, Calvin Penfold has the ball, he passes it to Brooks, who side passes it to Angelos and it is again reaches Hughes. He now puts a through ball into Smith, the former goalkeeper, now striker. He has a shot, the keeper saves it. Glass has the ball and he hits it back to the goal and Dorkchester are now two nil up. It is another great goal the Stevenage fans don't look impressed at all. They are being shown up by this small team town.

Stevenage have a shot on goal it is saved by Escobar. He now launches the ball up the field it is picked up by Brooks, who is running with the ball and now to Angelos. He is tackled and now Stevenage come away with it, they are trying to get a shot on the goal but they are being blocked at every moment by Elliot and Champman. The Dorkchester defence have been rock solid and are stopping them at every turn. Well, the referee has blown for the end of the first half and I can't quite believe it, but Dorkchester are on the verge of the FA cup third round. What is going to happen in the second half? Can Stevenage turn this around and get back into the tie?"

Logan and the team were all in the changing room. There was a buzz and they were ready for the second half. Logan called for the team's attention and addressed the team, "Okay team, We are half way to making history for this club we need to make sure that we don't drop our guard and we continue to put the pressure on them. They are going to come at us hard, and we need to make sure we continue to stand up to them. Who wants to have the chance to play against premier league or championship team? Do you want to try yourself against the very best?"

The team were pumped and ready to go and face the next half. They left the changing room Logan saw Mr Glass who slowly made his way out. Logan called after and then asked "What's the matter? You look scared to go out for the second half."

Glass looked at him and said "Well, my dad was able to come to the match and after the game we are going to go out for a meal. Ben and I will finally come clean about us being together and I also plan to propose to him at the end of the meal. I just have so much going on I'm scared and just wanted to pause before the start of the second half".

Logan put his arm around him and whispered in his ear, says "You are a remarkable man and I am proud and honoured to know you. You are a great footballer and apparently, a good teacher and if it your family can't accept it, then that is their loss. This team, this town accepts you for who you are. Now we need to get out for the second half."

The two of them catch up with the rest of the team Logan take his place on the bench next to Bob.

"Well both teams are out for the second half. Can Stevenage get back into this game or will Dorkchester reach the FA cup third round. Well, Stevenage kicks off and already there's a tackle from Rodgers, who is now flying down the left wing. He is being chased by Stevenage players, but they can't just keep up with, or get anywhere near him. He puts a cross in andMcFadden heads the ball at the goal but the keeper pushes it away. Now the ball comes out to Glass, who just hits the ball straight back at the goal. The keeper but diving it is just not able to reach it and Dorkchester are now three nil up. This team are on their way to the FA cup third round proper. Stevenage have made three changes, they have sent on three attacking players. Stevenage a team who have a history of their own of knocking out bigger

181

teams, but today, they look like they are going to be on the other end of upset. Stevenage are on the attack they put a cross in. Escobar catches the ball in mid-air and throws it out. Stevenage collect the ball and again put the ball into the box. Champman, the Tank clears the ball out, It's still of Stevenage's possession, they are sending the ball forward again, but still can't break down this Dorkchester defence. The final whistle goes and the match is over. Dorkchester FC are in the third round of the cup. Yes you heard me correctly. The small town of Dorkchester are going to be playing in the third round, Well, let's see who they get in next round. This team are creating miracles."

The team changed and headed to the pub, apart from Glass, who had to meet with his parents and Ben. Logan called out to him, "Good luck, I am proud of you."

Whilst the team enjoyed the celebration, Logan had a call from the producer of The One Show. They wanted Logan to come on the show, as they would be doing the draw for the third round of the cup and wanted to have Logan on their show for an interview. Logan accepted the invitation and they said they would arrange a car to pick him up.

Later that evening, Logan was enjoyed a cup of tea and watched TV when he heard a knock at his door. He jumped up from the armchair and opened the door, it was Stephen. Tears ran down his face and it looked as though he been punched in the face. Logan asked, "Wo, what the matter? What's happened?" Tesre still ran down his face. "My dad said that he was ashamed of me, he doesn't want anything to do with me, his gay son. He won't accept mine and Ben's marriage, he even punched me in the face and threatened to kill me if he ever saw me again, he told that me I have brought shame on him and his family."

Logan invited him in. They both went inside. Logan then

182

said "I am so sorry that you had to go through that and I am sorry how your dad treated you,"

Stephen replied, "Itisn't your fault I knew this day would come and deep down I knew this was how he would react. Now I can finally move on Ben and I can get married and live our lives as we want, no more secrets."

Logan looked at him and said "Look, I've have been invited to appear on The One Show, why don't you take my place and tell your story." Stephen response was, "It's okay, me and Ben just want to get married and enjoy the rest of our lives together but I have just come up with idea. I will have to clear it with Ben but would like, if it's okay with you, if before the cup match, me and Ben can get married on the pitch."

Logan smiled and hugged him and said, "It would be an honour for us to host the first FA cup wedding and it will be an amazing and memorable day."

The next day the Logan readied himself for his appearance on The One Show.

"We welcome our next guest he is the current manager of Dorkchester, a team who have surprised everyone by making into the FA cup third round and the draw that will be taking place shortly." Logan walked on the set and took a seat on the chair, "Welcome to the show Logan, so tell me, what is your secret? You have taken a team from nowhere into the third round of the cup."

Logan looked at the camera and said "Well, there is no secret, we are all just playing to our strengths, each player has shown their true talent." The host then asked "The team has also been in the papers for another reason, has this been good for the town?"

Logan replied, "The team and me are not frightened about

taking a stand for injustice and discrimination, The town of Dorkchester is open to all and I would like to invite you all to the first FA cup wedding, Stephen Glass and Ben White will getting married be before are third round FA cup match against whoever. who ever They will be getting married on the pitch."

The host then said, "Well, you certainly like to make a statement. That is a great show of respect to be able as a club to show your honour for the LGBT community and this will be a memorable match. This is truly special. We at The One Show would like to congratulate Stephen and Ben on their engagement and we will be honoured to attend the wedding. Well next up is the draw itself."

Dorkchester were drawn at home against Wigan Atheletic in the third round of the cup.

The Third Round of the Cup

One evening the team were training. Logan called over to McFadden, he had a parcel in his hand. He handed it to him and told him that his friend had made these noise defenders for his son and now his son would be able to come to the cup match and see him score. McFadden gave him a huge hug and tears ran down his face, they were tears of joy. They heard a commotion and and saw cops and they were handcuffing Escobar and Cesar. Logan and McFadden rushed over and Logan started shouting at the policeman "What is going on? Why are you arresting my players?" Captain Rodgers appeared. One of the policeman and said, "Sorry, but we have had reports that Escobar and Cesar are both here a illegally and we need to take them to station to answer some questions. We are sorry for disturbing your training but I have to do my job, I can't make any exceptions for anyone." Rover then pushed his dad and screamed at him, "Dad you can't do this." But the two players were lead away in handcuffs and put into the awaiting police cars.

Logan turned to the team and told them, "That is a wrap for training today. I need to make a call." Logan went to his office and dialled a number on his phone. He spoke to the person on the other end of the phone and he told them that he needed him to come to Dorkchester he needed his help and would give him the full details when he arrived.

Logan went to the police station, he asked the desk sergeant if he could speak to his players. Captain Rodgers gave him permission. The first person he saw was Escobar, he was in an interview room. He sat down at the table and spoke to Escobar, "How are they treating you? Tell me everything, the whole truth." Escobar responded, with "I snuck into England with no papers. I wanted to find work to earn enough so I can bring my family to England. The hardest thing that I have done was leaving them but I needed to find work I have been in England for three years and have almost got enough to bring them to live with me. In my country, I was a Doctor but when civil war broke out, my hospital was blown up and I was not able to work. I needed to do what was the best for my family." Logan looked into his eyes and asked him, "Why did you not seek asylum?"

Escobar then told him "I met Mr Smith and Mr Sharpe and they offered me a job and told me not to worry about all that, they would make sure I was okay and didn't need to worry about anything." Logan hit hand on the table and then told him. "Look I will help you and make sure that they don't send you home. I have got somebody coming to help with your case trust me I won't let you down." He shook his hand before leaving the room and headed next door to the other interview room

In the next room sat Cesar. Logan sat down and asked Cesar the same question "How are you being treated? Yo need tell me everything and the truth."

Cesar looked up and shook his head at first, but then he started to speak. "I was a soldier in the Civil war but I just couldn't do it anymore. I could not kill my fellow man. So I deserted and ran away, if I was ever to return to my country I would be killed. The tyrant who is in charge imposed martial law. I have no family, no friends but I couldn't kill anymore, it just isn't who I am, I can't return, they will kill me. Please you must help me, please save me."

Logan looked at him straight in his eyes and Logan then said, "Trust me Cesar I won't let them take you back. I have my best man coming, he is on the way and we will help you."

Logan gave Cesar a hug and gave him tissues because Cesar was crying. Logan could see the fear in his eyes, he just looked petrified.

Later that evening Logan got a knock at his door, when he opened it up there was Mr Sharpe. He had some papers in his hand. "Good evening Logan, I'm sorry to hear about your players being arrested. I have an offer for you."

Logan looked at him standing in his doorway and said to him, "Look buddy, whatever you are selling, I am not interested."

Mr Sharpe replied, "Selling, I'm not selling I want to buy. Look, we all know that you don't want to be festering in this town and I can make that happen. I will buy the pub and this rundown cottage and you can move on. If you agree to sell to me, I will make sure your little friends are able to stay. You see I know people who can make it go away. What do you say?"

Logan laughed and told him straight, "You're a funny man." Mr Sharpe looked puzzled, Logan carried on, "Wait, you're serious, you want me to sell my uncle's pub to you? What do you want with the pub? Mr Sharpe said to him, "I don't want the pub, I just don't want you in my club and I can help you to leave quicker and if you leave, I can bring my son back to the club."

Logan was about to close the door and said to Mr Sharpe, "Now you listen to me. I have no intention of selling to you. I am starting to like this town I may not sell and just stay forever."

Mr Sharpe was angry with this response and he put his foot in front of the door to stop Logan from closing it and he screamed in Logan's face. "You will regret this I own this town, everyone works for me. I will make you regret this."

Logan then pushed his foot from the door and slammed the door shut in his face. A few days later Logan was waiting at the café for someone, a man came in. He was dressed in a suit and tie looking very important he takes a seat at the table with Logan and shake his hand. Logan then speaks to the man "Glad you could come now let's get down to business I have two friends who have been accused of being here illegally and have been arrested, Raul Esocbar has come to England from a warzone to help find funds so that he can bring his family over. He was a doctor in his country and has been working at the biscuit factory and then Cesar, who is a former soldier, who could not deal with killing anymore and escaped the frontline. If he was to return, he would be killed and finally, there is Mr Sharpe, who seems to have some sort of hold on this town and wants me to sell to him."

The guy sat up straight and he told Logan "I will represent your players and will do everything to stop them from being sent back, leave that with me. As for Mr Sharpe, I am well aware of him this man and I have already had one of my agents go undercover to find out what they can on him. Let me tell you, this guy has his dirty hands in everything, I have been made aware that the biscuit factory was struggling with massive debts and after Mr Smith made a deal with your Mr Sharpe, they were wiped out overnight and a few weeks later your players and six others started working at the Factory and when my agent tried to find information on these, he found fake passports and papers for them and hundreds more. It appears that Mr Smith and Mr Sharpe have been working together. But the most interesting part that my agent discovered was that your Mr Sharpe has plans to replace the football stadium and build a huge new supermarket in its place. It looks like he had plans for the team to continue to lose and amount massive debts so he could buy it and knock it down, wiping the club out of existence."

Logan stood up and looked at the guy in the face and said, "You have my permission to do whatever you can to make sure these players are able to play in the third round of the cup. I think I need to have a word with Mr Smith." The two shook hands and Logan left the café.

Logan got into a taxi and went to the biscuit factory, he saw the receptionist at the desk said that Harvey has asked him to pick up something for him from his office. She let him in without signing in. Once Logan was in the factory, he went straight to the main office and he barged into the office. Mr Smith sat at his desk speaking on the phone. He looked up and saw Logan standing in front of him, He then asked Logan, "Logan, what the hell?"

Logan then screamed, "Tell me the truth. What deal do you have with Mr Sharpe and how does this affect my players?"

Mr Smith said, "I have no idea what you are talking about."

Logan looked at him straight in the face. Logan then said, "Don't be coy with me, I know that you were in massive debt and then suddenly, overnight, it was wiped out and you then employed these illegals. Also, why does your buddy have plans to build a new superstore in place of the Dorkchester Club."

Mr Smith put the phone down and then said, "Look Logan, it is my business. I had to do what I could to save my family business, I nearly lost everything. I couldn't let my son down. So, when Mr Sharpe came to me and offered me money, all I had to do was employ a few people that he sent over, without any questions. I couldn't refuse but you must be mistaken about the supermarket, this was never part of the deal, his son was a part of the team."

Logan laughed at him and said, "You made a deal with the Devil and he now owns you. I think you should have read the

189

small print to see what he actually wanted from you, because you been screwed."

Logan turned and left the office, as he came out of the office he saw Harvey. Harvey asked what was wrong, Logan told him to ask his dad. As Logan left, he looked back and sawMr Smith on the phone and he was screamed down the phone and Logan could see Harvey also shouting at his dad.

Later that evening, at training the team were very depressed and lethargic and were not interesting in training but then Mr Smith and Harvey came over to them and called all the players and Logan over. Harvey said, "My dad has something to say to you all, how he has let us down." Mr Smith started to speak, "I just want to say that I am sorry. My intention was to save my business. I made a deal with Mr Sharpe and in order to clear my debts, I sold the ground to him. I always thought he loved the club, like me and loved having it here. Now Mr Sharpe has told me that due to the team being the worst club ever and is losing money. He intends to shut the club down and build a new superstore in its place."

The players were all shouted, "What the hell, Holy shit, he can't do this."

"Look, I am so sorry but there is nothing I can do. Once this season is over, so will the club."

Logan then spoke to the players. "Look team, I have no intention of letting this happen. I have my best man working on getting the players back in time for the cup match and if we continue to keep winning in the cup and get a huge team and we will have the world watching, maybe we can save the club. We are Dorkchester. we are Dorkchester. we are Dorkchester."

The rest of the team joined in, chanting We are Dorkchester we are Dorchester. Harvey turned to his dad and told him, "I am ashamed of you, but I and the team will save this team. We are Dorkchester. We are Dorkchester."

A week passed and Logan met up with at the jail with Cesar, Escobar and the smartly dressed man. They were in a large meeting room, along with Captain Rodgers and another man. The smartly dressed man spoke, "Okay, now I want you to release my client as they have wrongly been detained." Captain Rodgers then said, "Your clients are illegal immigrants and broke the law and have forged papers to stay in this country." The smartly dressed gentleman then said "Allegedly here illegally, but I have proof that these allegations are false." He then pulled out a huge folder and laid it on the table. "Firstly let's start with Escobar, I have proof that he is studying so that he can get his qualifications to become a Doctor in this country. He is also working part time at the factory."

He pushed the paperwork in front of Captain Rodgers. Rodgers and the other guy sitting next to him looked and read what had been placed in front of them and then Captain Rodgers said "With the evidence presented to us, we have no grounds for arrest and all charges are dropped." Escobar put his hand on his head, relieved that he is free to stay, The the smartly dressed man carried on speaking, but there was a knock on the door. "Let us move onto Cesar now. This is a man who has seen and done things that will scar him for his life. Yet with all these scars, he managed to find love." The door opened and this young woman who wore a short red dress and black top came running in. She went straight over to Cesar and put her arms around him. He carried on talking, "Let me introduce you to Chantelle, Cesar's fiancée and she is carrying his baby."

Chantelle said, "Please don't take my love from me, Please

191

don't take my baby's daddy away, please I beg you. If he goes home, they will kill him, please don't kill my man. I love him with all my heart. He is my soul mate." Captain Rodger and the other man started talking between themselves and then looked up and Captain Rodgers said, "We have decided to drop all charges and will seek asylum for Cesar due to the risk to life."

The room erupted in joy and Chantelle kissed Cesar on the lips. The smartly dressed man and Logan shook hands with Captain Rodger and the other man as they left the room. Chantelle held Cesar's hand and Escobar cried. Logan then said to smartly dressed man, "Thank you for your help. Just one question though, who is Chantelle?" The smartly dressed man said, "Look, it's a pleasure, it isn't often I get to do something good and lets just say Chantelle is, well, let's just say she charges by the hour."

"Have to say she even convinced me that she loved him." Logan laughed and said, "I owe you."

A few days later was the FA Cup match.

Before the cup match the team were all dressed in their suits and ties. Stephen paced around the room, he was nervous. Logan approached him and asked, "How are you doing?"

He replied, "Boss, I am more nervous about getting married today that having to face Wigan later. Am I doing the correct thing? Am I putting a target on my back? It is not easy being gay and a footballer, now the whole world will know and I'm also putting Ben into the limelight." Logan looked into his eyes and said, "Love is more important than anything, Ben loves you and you love ben, this is far more important than anything I have to say. I am jealous of you. Love, you have found it. I can't get close to people and have never truly been in love, I am so happy for you."

Stephen smiled and hugged Logan, then said "Logan can I ask a favour?"

Logan replied, "Anything." Stephen asked if Logan would walk him down the aisle as his dad isn't coming to the wedding. Logan, without hesitation, said it would be his honour to give him away. Logan walked him down the aisle and as he walked down with him, he looked over and saw Mcfaden's son smiling away, wearing his ear defenders. Once Logan had done his duty he sat down on the chairs that were laid out on the pitch. Logan sat in the chair next to Lucy. Ben and Stephen said their vows and kissed each other in the centre circle. Logan had noticed that Lucy had put her hand on his and they were holding hands as the wedding was completed. She quickly pulled it away when it was over and gave Logan a smile as they left the pitch. As the team left the pitch Stephen said, "That was the hard bit done, now let's go and beat Wigan in the cup."

"We are live at Dorkchester, who have been the surprise package in the cup. We were also treated, before this match, to the first cup wedding, as one Stephen Glass married his partner Ben White live on the pitch, this is truly a breakthrough for football and hopefully opens up doors for others. Dorkchester have been standing up for LGBT community, not only did they support their player, who is a Drag artist, but opened up their doors to having an openly gay wedding on the pitch. Well, let's get to the action Dorkchester are playing at home and are facing the Former FA cup winners Wigan. Can the team pull off another upset and reach the fourth round of the cup. The team are coming out and the game gets underway. Wigan kick off and send the ball forward, they get a shot on goal and Escobar pushes it away. Wigan come again, they are through one on one with the keeper and Escobar again pulls off another save. So far, it has all been Wigan in the opening fifteen minutes and the score is still nil nil due to the Dorkchester keeper, who has pulled of a few good saves. Wigan again with another shot on goal and again Escobar is there to pull off another fine save. Every time Dorkchester get the ball up the field, it is coming back at them. They have their keeper to thank for keeping them in this tie.

We are coming up to half time and the tie is still locked at nil nil there have been no shots on goal from Dorkchester, it has been Wigan all the way."

The team were in the changing room at half time and were taking their refreshments, when Logan stood on the medical bench, almost lost his balance, and shouted to get their attention, "What the fuck was that? Look, you stop kissing these players arses and show them who we are, We are Dorkchester. We are Dorkchester. We are Dorkchester."

The rest of the team started to chant, until the whole changing room vibrated from the sound of the chanting. The team continued chanting until they got onto the pitch.

"Welcome back to the tie between Wigan and Dorkchester. So far it has all been Wigan. There has not been anything from the Dorkchester team, can they turn it round and make a real game of it? Straight from the kick off McFadden has the ball, he gets a shot on the goal but the keeper puts it over the bar and Dorkchester have a corner. Already in the second half Dorkchester have done more than they did in the whole first half. The ball is crossed, Cesar gets a head on it, he has scored! Dorkchester have scored from the corner, he was left unmarked in the area and just headed the ball into the goal. I can't believe that Dorkchester are going to do it again. They are leading Wigan. How are Wigan going to turn this round and get the ball passed the Dorkchester keeper, who has been on fire today? Wigan are coming forward and the ball is passed into the penalty area. Champman takes out the striker, that has got to be a penalty, Wigan have just been given a chance to get back onto level terms and they can turn this tie around.

The ball is placed onto the penalty spot, he hits it cleanly and it's a fingertip save from Escobar, who pushes the ball away from the goal. Dorkchester get away with it and they are still one up. They could be on the way to the fourth round. Wigan has thrown everything at Dorkchester but they have been up to the task. The ref is looking at his watch and he puts it up to his lips, Dorkchester are into the draw for the fourth round. The fairy-tale is not over and this team have shown they have no fear of whoever has to come down to Dorkchester. Well, until the next time, we leave you with another view of the goal that sent Dorkchester into the fourth round."

The team were all in the pub, Logan sat on a table on his own. Lucy came over with a beer and sat next to him and said, "Why are you not celebrating with the others?" Logan looked at her and smiled, then said, "Lucy, I just want to say I am sorry, I didn't mean to hurt you, when I am with you and talking with you, I feel happy. I am not used to this and I have been with many women before."

Lucy said, "This isn't something I want to hear about, your conquests."

Logan replied, "Sorry. What I am trying to say is, I feel differently when I am with you, there's something special about

195

you, I didn't want to ruin it by fucking you and losing you."

Lucy smiled and then said "Oh well, I'm glad that you didn't want to sleep with me because I am ugly, but it's because you need to figure yourself out. Look I like you Logan and you made me feel amazing and we had perfect date until you left me in my underwear."

Lucy kissed Logan on lips and said, "Logan, if you want to be with me, I am not going anywhere. But don't leave me waiting too long, I might get other offers." She kissed him again, They were interrupted by Smith and Rodgers screaming, we are playing Bolton. We are Dorkchester the mighty Dorkchester.

Chapter 12

The Fourth Round

The town was al abuzz with the prospect of the fourth round cup tie. But there was one person who wasn't that happy about how much press the club had received. It may impact on his plans to close the club and build his new superstore. Mr Sharpe had made arrangements to set up a meeting with Harvey and in this meeting. Mr Sharpe tried to blackmail Harvey, to make sure they lost the next cup match. If he didn't he would recall all his dad's debts and this would mean the closure of the factory. He needed to think about the hundreds of jobs that would be lost just because of a football match. He also informed him that he had details of his dad illegally hiring immigrants and this would be passed onto the police and his dad would be arrested and face prison.

After this meeting, Harvey was unsure of what to do. On one hand he had his family and friends, and on the other, he had his teammates and the town. Harvey rushed over to see Logan and seek advice. He arrived at Logan's house and when Logan let him in, he could see that he was very distressed. Logan sat him down in the chair and told him to take a breath. He then asked him, "What is the matter?" Smith explained everything. "Mr Sharpe says that I need to make sure we get knocked out of the cup and if I don't make this happen, he is going to take back the money that my dad owes him, from when he saved the factory. He also says he has details of my dad's illegal deals and he could face jailtime. This would destroy him. He'd lose factory and with it, all the jobs. I am telling you this because I can't let my team down. You and the club are also my family. What can we do Logan?"

Logan took him by the arm and pulled him into him and gave him a hug. Logan took his phone, dialled a number and told the person on the phone, "I have a new job for you." Once he had finished on the phone he told Harvey not to worry, he will sort it out but he needed to call Harvey's dad and arrange a meeting with him, his dad and Mr Sharpe.

Two days after this Logan and Harvey drove up to the factory where the arranged meeting was taking place. Once they were in the factory, they headed into a meeting room. In the room, sat the long black table, were Mr Sharpe and Tony the top end and Mr Smith was sat at the middle. Logan and Harvey sat at the other end. Mr Sharpe looked up smiled and said, "Shall we get started?" Logan told him to slow his roll, they were still waiting for one more representative. A few minutes later Logan's friend, the smartly dressed man, came into the room, sat down next to him, and passed him some papers.

Logan then started the meeting "I'd like to thank all parties for attending today. So let's get started. The first order of business is the money that Smith owes Sharpe." (The smartly dressed man stood up, and walked up to Mr Sharpe placed a cheque in front of him) Logan continued, "this cheque,? with a few extra pennies, will cover the debt owed to you."

Mr Sharpe looked at the cheque, then threw it down on the table and said, "You think you can just buy me out and I will walk away. I will shut this factory down and all your workers will be unemployed, how will this affect this town? It will be all your fault."

Logan told him. "I don't think so. You see, the factory has just had a change in how it is run.

The company is now on the stock market and each member of staff has shares in the company, There also has been restructure of the board and it is under new management."

Harvey stood up and said, "We would like to inform you, that your services are no longer needed." Mr Sharpe was angry, he lobbed a bottle across the room and screamed, "I will get you for this. I have friends in the police. who will shut you down and Smith. you and your son will rot in jail. This isn't over." The smartly dressed man walked over and placed another pile of papers in front of Sharpe, who looked at them, turned to Tony and said, "We must go." Tony said, "But dad, we can't back down now, I want my club back."

But Mr Sharpe just screamed, "It's over, we must go now."

They left the room, there was uproar of cheers. Mr Smith thanked Logan and asked what had been shown to Mr Sharpe. Logan smiled and just said "He isn't the only one who has friends in high, okay maybe, low places, but I don't think he will be bothering us again."

Mr Smith said "Well whatever you did, I am glad you did, you have saved this factory and this town."

Dorkchester FC's league form had actually started to pick up and they had won two matches and drawn three before their fourth round cup match.

"Here we are then on a cold wet day. How is this muddy pitch going to hold out in this weather? We have the giant killers, Dorkchester, facing Bolton, a former giant of the game. Will Dorkchester's journey finally end here or can they pull off another upset? The rain is coming down and we are just under way. Bolton are on the attack, the pitch is very muddy. How will the Bolton players cope on this pitch? Bolton have a shot, Escobar dives to his right and he has his gloves on the ball. He launches it up the field and Rodgers has the ball, he taps it to Brooks, who finds McFadden in a space and who slides it to Smith, the former keeper now striker, and he hits a shot on goal. He hits the crossbar and it rebounds out and Bolton get the ball away. Bolton are coming for another attack, the rain is starting to come down harder. Bolton have another shot, it soars past the goal and out for a goal k. Escobar launches the ball from the goal kick, it's headed on by McFadden and Smith volleys it, the Bolton keep is unable to reach it and it is in the back of the net. What a strike, this team have done it again and with a goal that is as good as any I've seen, by Smith, a player who looks comfortable on the ball and could probably do a good job in the lower league of the football pyramid. If he continues to perform like this I am sure he will be getting offers. We are coming up to the thirty eighth minute and Dorkchester are one nil up and as we reach half time Bolton have had very few shots on goal, they tested the keeper early on, but did not trouble him too much after that. They are going to have to do more in the second half. The whistle goes and that is the end of the first half. I still can't believe it, but Dorkchester FC are on the eve of possibly making into the fifth round draw. The referee ends the half."

"We are back and what can Bolton do differently in this half? The rain is still falling and the pitch is like a big. Can. the Bolton players get used to playing on this pitch, which is very different from that of the one they are used to. Bolton have a long range shot, but this soars over the goal, not even close. Bolton again

200

come with the ball, they hit another shot, this goes flying over the crossbar, Bolton are just not able to get the ball on target. They are not troubling the keeper., Brooks has picked up the ball he now clips the ball up to McFadden, he has a shot, the keeper makes a good save. Bolton get the ball up the field, they hit another shot and Escobar pushes it over the bar. A corner for Bolton, they hit the ball into the busy penalty area and there is a lot of hustle and bustle. Oh no, the ball is the back of the net. From the relay, it appears to have come off Champman and that's an own goal. The game is now locked at one all. Is this the turning point in the tie, can Bolton go on and get the winner or will Dorkchester pull of another goal from their bag of tricks. Rodgers has the ball, he is running down the wing, he launches the ball to Penfold, one of the twins, who then crosses the high ball to McFadden. He's been brought down, that has to be a penalty, The ref has pointed to the spot for Dorkchester. Champman picks up the ball, it looks like he is going to try and make amends for his own goal. Champman places the ball on the spot, he's hit the ball, oh my, the power in that straight down the middle. It almost ripped the netting from the goal. The power in that shot! The keeper had no chance and Dorkchester are again in front. The team are leading two one and we are going to the late stages of the match. Can Bolton come back again. Bolton are trying everything they can to get another equalizer but they are not getting anything from the Dorkchester defence, they are holding them at a bay, The ref ends the match and Bolton have been knocked out by the team from Dorkchester. At the start of the season, nobody had heard of this team and now they are in the third round of the cup. Well, this team are making history every time they take to the field. I don't think even if they had to face a premier league team, they would fear them."

201

The team again celebrated at the pub. The draw was being televised and they waited to see who they would play next. The whole pub fell silent for the draw. Dorkchester were drawn at home again, they seemed to have had the luck in getting home ties. The whole pub gasped when saw that they that they would face Fulham. There were cheers and drinks were thrown in the air would they be able to pull off another upset they will be in the quarterfinals of the FA cup.

Chapter 13

Fifth Round

A couple of days after the cup match Logan relaxed at home, he had a free day. There was a knock at the door, Lucy stood there with a picnic bag and asked, "Would you like to go for a walk with me, we can have a picnic together. No strings attached, just as friends?"

Logan gave her a smile and winked and replied, "I would love to join you for a walk."

He grabbed his keys and coat and locked the door and joined Lucy a walk. She took him to the woods that were behind the cottage. They walked up the hill together and stopped. Lucy stood at the top of the hill and asked Logan to join her, He stood next to her they both look out and you can see the whole town from the view and just in the distance. They could just make out the factory and the stadium. Logan said, "Wow, this is a wonderful view of the town, it just looks so peaceful." Lucy told him, "I like to come up here and just enjoy the silence. Pub life can get a little noisy sometimes and I just like being up here and looking at the town that saved me, and being thankful for it." They sat on the picnic blanket and enjoyed the food that Lucy had prepared for them. They have ham and cheese sandwiches with crisps and she had made some scones and there was homemade jam. Logan told her that she had made a very nice spread and he thanked her for showing him the view. He said he would have to make sure that he came back when life got too hectic, just to enjoy the peace. After they had finished their picnic, they packed up and headed back down the hill. As they walked down Lucy tripped over a log and lost her balance, but Logan had his wits about him and caught her and stopped her from falling to the ground. Lucy smiled and look at him and said, "Good catch."

Logan laughs and said "Well, it isn't every day that a beauty falls into my arms."

Lucy laughed and said "Hey, none of that charm, we are just friends. This is not date."

Logan said "Yes, whatever you say. Well, as we are friends and don't know if you would be interested but me and the team are going to a wrestling show to see the Tank compete for the heavyweight championship belt. I am inviting you as friend not as date."

Lucy replied "Of course I would like to join you and team watching the Tank fight and win the title."

Logan smiled and he thanks Lucy for a lovely afternoon. He would see her in the week and pick her up for the wrestling.

It was the day of the wrestling match and the team had a mini bus organised. Logan was dressed in black jeans. He had been on the wrestling website and bought Tank merchandise, so he wore a black shirt that had a picture of the Tank slamming another wrestler to the ground. The word Tank was highlighted in green. He went to the pub and went up to find Lucy. As he knocked on the door of her room above the pub, she called for him come in and asked for his help. Logan came in and saw Lucy, wearing a long black dress, Logan asked her, "Don't you think you're overdressed for a wrestling show."

Lucy gave him a cheeky grin and said "Well you never know

who you might meet at a wrestling show. Hey, I might meet one of those big, hunky wrestlers and they can pick me up and whisk me a way." Logan replied, "Fair enough." The mini bus was outside waiting for them and when the team saw Lucy, they wolf whistled and cheered as she entered the bus. Logan said, at the top of his voice, "Now let's not look like a pack of animals. Save it for the show."

Lucy sat next to Logan they were in front row. The Tank had reserved seats for them all. The wrestling started. There was an opening match between just two wrestlers. Lucy really enjoyed watching the wrestlers flying around the ring. The first match lasted fifteen minutes. The second match was an all-woman match. The female villain at one point, sat on Logan's lap and ran her hand through his hair. Lucy didn't like this and was cross, but was happy when the other wrestler came and smacked the villain in the face. A smile could be seen on Lucy's face. The woman's match lasted twenty minutes. The third match was a tag match and after the tag match there was a half time interval. In the break Logan asked Lucy if she wanted a drink. She said she would have a coke. Logan came back with drinks and they talked while they waited for the second half. Logan asked "How are you enjoying the show? Are you enjoying seeing the wrestlers in their tight lycra."

Lucy looked up at him and said, "Well not as much as you were, I'm surprised that you didn't get her number." Logan replied, "Don't tell me you are jealous?"

Lucy snapped back, "Jealous of her? Look, remember this is no date and we are only friends." before they could continue Rodgers and Smith came over. They had bought some foam hands and had been drinking, so were a little merry. One said, "Boss, you enjoying the show? Hey boss, looks like you got a lap dance, you lucky man." Logan glared at them both and they sat down on the chairs. There were another three matches before the match they had all been waiting for.

The ring announcer introduced the Championship contenders.

"Ladies and gentleman, boys and girls. We now have the main event of the evening. Weighing in at twelve stone, we have your British wrestling heavyweight champion, give it up for the the Doc Father." The lights flickered and the room erupted with boo and cheers and the Doc father entered the ring. carrying his championship belt over his shoulders. He was dressed in a doctor's jacket and under his jacket it looked like he was dressed as a gangster. He climbed into the ring and held the belt aloft and then ring announcer called out. "And the challenger, weighing thirteen stone, the football superstar, we give you the Tank."

Everyone stood to clap cheer the Tank, who was dressed in his Dorkchester football kit. Tank walked down to the ring, high fiving everyone that he walked past, When he saw his teammates he gave a grand smile, then climbed into the ring. He stood facing the crowd, holding his arms in the air but as soaked up the atmosphere, he was attacked by the Doc Father who shoulder barged him from behind and the referee signalled to sound the bell to start the match.

The Doc Father picked Tank up and slap him across the face. He then threw him into the ring ropes. As Tank came flying from the ropes, the Doc father Just stood there and they just collided. Neither moved.Doc father then went for a test of strength, he held his right arm in the air and Tank put his hands into the grip position. The Doc Father took advantage and kneed him in the midriff and Tank dropped down to his knees. The Doc father then ran, with full head of steam, and dropped his elbow on the back

206

of Tank's head. This took Tank down to the mat, this led to Doc Father stamping on Tank as he is on the floor. The crowd hissed and booed The Doc Fathers antics, He then picked up Tank and slammed him down to the floor. Doc Father then looked at the crowd as he had the Tank down on the floor, he was heard to say, "Is this your challenger? He is nothing." The Doc Father stood on the top rope and he is at the top he goes too jump on top of the Tank ready to drop his elbow, but as The Doc Father jumped, the Tank was able to move out of the way. The Tank then pulled himself up and as the two wrestlers stare each other down, The Tank chopped the Doc Father, grabbed him, picked him and Supplex him to the floor. He followed this move with a drop on top of the Doc Father. He tried to go for the pin but only managed to get the count of two, The Tank then picked up the Doc Father and tried to slam him down but the Doc Father rake him in the eye, The Doc farther quickly rolled out of the ring and tried to catch his breath. The Tank followed him out to the ring side. As Tank moved close to the Doc, the Doc punched him in his midriff and rammed him into the ring post, The Doc rolled the Tank into the ring and stomped away as the The Tank is on the floor. The Doc then went for his finishing move. He put his arms around the Tank's throat and locked him in a chicken wing lock. The Tank rolled and got his hand to the rope and the Doc had to release the hold. The Tank stood up and The Doc is charged at him and went for the spear but missed and took out the ref. Then out of nowhere, the Doc's assistant, who had been banned from ringside, jumped into the ring holding the belt and it looked like he was going to hit the Tank with the belt, but instead he clobbered the Doc with it. He ripped off his nurse's uniform and beneath it was a shirt saying 'sergeant in arms' He then slid out of the ring. The Tank then picked up the Doc and slammed him to the floor. He set up for his finishing move, the sliding tackle. He placed his opponent in the corner and he then ran from the opposite corner and dropkicked him. This laid the Doc Father flat out on the floor. He rolled on top of the Doc pinning him down and the ref counted one, two, three. The crowd didn't know whether to boo or cheer as the ring announcer called out, "Your new British heavyweight champion, the Tank."

The referee handed Tank the belt, as the 'Sergeant in arms' came in and hugged the Tank. They hold the belt aloft in the ring. The Tank left the ring but unlike his entry, he does not acknowledge the crowd at all, walked past everyone and left to the crowd's boos. Lucy told Logan that she had enjoyed the wrestling show and Logan said that next time he would make sure she got an invite Logan added, "Anytime you want to wrestle just let me know." Lucy didn't look impressed with this comment and shook her head.

Later that evening, the whole team were at the pub celebrating with the champ. They all posed with the belt, even Lucy and Logan posed with the belt. They celebrated the evening with booze and belts. As the evening died down, just Lucy and Logan were left in the bar. Lucy said good night to Logan but before he left he lent in and kissed her on her lips and he said "I am sorry about our date. I really like you, if you would let me, can we try again." Lucy pulled away from him but didn't say anything and just pushed him away. Logan left the pub.

The next weekend was the match against Fulham Sadly the Tank unable to play, but before the match he walked around the pitch showing off his gold.

"We welcome you to the fifth round of the cup. We are here at Dorkchester, whose opponents are Fulham. We had interesting pre match event, as the Dorkchester player, better known as the Tank, a part time footballer, part time factory worker, paraded around with his Championship belt. I don't know where he finds the time to fit it all in. How much will Tank be missed in the heart of Dorkchester's defence, as he currently injured after winning the wrestling title and will this give Fulham the chance in the match. Cesar steps into the captain's place. Well let's get ready for slam down, let's hope none of the players try any wrestling moves on the field today. We are under way and Fulham have the ball. They have the ball down the wing and have put in the ball into the box and Cesar takes the ball off the striker's feet. What a good tackle! He feeds the ball to Calvin Penfold, who runs with it but he is tackled and Fulham come away with the ball. They are just on the edge of the box, they take the shot goal butat it is tipped over by Escobar. The corner is crossed in and the Escobar clutches the ball from the air. He rolls the ball out but it is intercepted by Fulham, they take another shot, but safe hands by Escobar stop it going in the net. The Dorkchester team have to thank their keeper for keeping them in the tie as he has pulled off save after save. Hold on, Rodgers has the ball, he is running with it, he was fed by Escobar who found him in space. Just a punt up the field the ball is in the penalty area, McFadden has the ball, he is taking it around the keeper but he is taken out by the keeper, that has to be a penalty, The referee points to the spot and he has just shown the Fulham keeper the red card. Fulham are down to ten men and they have a penalty to defend, the Fulham have to substitute their keeper. McFadden places the ball on the spot, he takes a few steps back and takes small run up and kicks it and it hits the back of the net. Dorkchester are leading Fulham one nil, and Fulham down to ten men, They have a mountain to climb in the second half to save this tie. The ref brings the first half to a

209

close and there is a lot pushing and shoving between the Fulham players, they don't look happy at all."

In the changing room Logan told his team that they needed to stay calm in the second half, Fulham would everything at them to get back into the tie, but they needed to stick together as a team and make history by reaching the quarterfinals of FA Cup. Again they chanted, "We are Dorkchester. Weare Dorkchester."

"We are back for this FA cup match between Dorkchester and Fulham and we have had a very interesting first half. Fulham who are down to ten men and are one nil down. Can they level up this tie or will the giant killers Dorkchester pull of another upset and book their place in the quarterfinal of the FA cup? The ref blows to start the second half and Cesar has the ball, he launches the ball up field to Smith who is holding the ball up and he passes it to McFadden. The Fulham defence get a tackle in and come away with the ball. They get a shot on goal but again Escobar is up to the challenge and the Fulham strikers are not able to get past the Dorkchester keeper, with all their shots he has been up to the task, With Fulham needing to get back into the game they are making a change and taking of another defender and sending on another striker. Will this leave space for the Dorkchester team to take advantage of it. Logan has done wonders with this team, a team, who at the start of season had not won a single match until they started in the cup and they have done wonders, This team will be remembered for years to come as the non-league team that shocked the FA cup competition and truly brought the magic back to the cup. Fulham have the ball and are coming back at the Dorkchester goal and they feed the ball through and the striker is able to take the shot and it is the same story, the keeper is there again. The Dorkchester fans are starting to believe that they are minutes away from the FA cup quarter final match. The ref looks at his watch as Dorkchester punts the ball up the field. The ref blows the whistle and there is a pitch invasion. The few hundred Dorkchester fans that are at the ground, are running and hugging the players and Logan the manager, I can't quite believe it myself but Dorkchester are in the quarterfinals. Who ever said the magic of the FA cup has gone, need to follow this story. I wouldn't be surprised if Hollywood come calling, I wonder who will be playing me in the movie? Well I don't know about you but I will be watching with excitement for the draw to see who Dorkchester get in the quarterfinals. Well, I will see you next time. My final words are this is what make the FA cup so special."

The fans and the players did a lap of honour as the Fulham players left the field. They all chanted: "We are Dorchester. Wr are Dorkchester we are Dorkchester."

The team headed to the pub after the match and celebrated their huge achievement all night long.

The next day there was Logan's door. At the door and it was Mr Sharpe and his lawyer. Mr Sharpe said "Good Morning Logan. We have come to make you a final offer and as you will see, we have made you offer that is far more than either is worth."

Logan then replied with "Morning. I see you have brought the suit with you. Well let me say, so that you both hear, I will never sell anything to you and just so to be clear and so you understand, I also no longer own the pub, so it is not mine to sell." Mr Sharpe whispered into his lawyers ear and then said to Logan "Logan come on, let's be reasonable. If you take our deal, you can finally return to London. We all know about your financial issues. This will set you back up and you can finally go home.

This dream that you brought to the town and the club will end and the town will once again go back to the way it was before you were ever here. This is my town and nothing will stop me from closing down your little club and opening up my new superstore."

Logan gets right into his face and screamed, "No, Fucking. Deal."

Before Mr Sharpe said anymore, Logan closed the door. Logan heard Mr Sharpe shouting, "You will be sorry, I will make you pay, I own this town, I will make sure you get nothing, you will be sorry." Logan answered a call on his phone and from the other end heard, "We have got Everton, we are playing a premier league team in the quarterfinal and it is Everton."

Chapter 12

Quarter Finals and Semi-Final and Return to Playing

During a training session in the build-up to the cup matches Logan wanted to practise free kicks, he pulled the Tank to one side and he asked the defenders to set up a wall, asked McFadden to lay down on the ground behind the wall.

He then said to Tank, "Okay, a lot of teams try this in defending free kicks. What I want you to practise doing is, instead of going over the wall, I want you to aim for the players midriff. I want you to put full power into it and hit it as hard as you can, but in a game, when you do it, I want you to do it twice, after you have hit the player full pelt in the chest twice, the wall won't jump, they will think you will do it again, so on the third attempt, you hit it into the top corner." But before they could practise this drill one of the loyal fans ran over and shouted, "The pub is on fire! Quick! The pub is on fire." They rushed to their cars, Logan jumped in with Harvey and they rushed over to the pub. When they got there the fireman where already dousing the fire with their hoses.

Logan got out of the car and tried to rush into the pub. He was held back, he called for Lucy. One of the fireman came up to Logan and said, "Look son, let my men do their job. We don't need any heroes until they have made it safe."

Logan looked at Harvey and said to him, "But what about Lucy, I can't lose her as well. She is magical and special I have feelings for her that I have never had in my life."

Then Logan was tapped on his shoulder, he turned around to see who it was. he Lucy stood in front of him. Lucy then told Logan, "Well, I didn't know you cared." Logan did not say anything, he put his hands on her face and drew her lips to his and he kissed her. The smell of smoke hovered in the air but Logan and Lucy did not care as they kissed each other. They only stopped when the fireman came back over and told them that there was a small amount of damage but nothing that couldn't be repaired. Logan looked at Lucy and said, "I will kill Sharpe, this was him." Logan asked Harvey to drive him to the Sharpe house, Harvey did not want to do this because of how angry Logan was, but Logan said he would drop him for the cup match. So Harvey gave in and took him to the Sharpe house.

Logan was banging on the door of the house and screamed, "Get out here now."

The door suddenly opened and Mrs Sharpe was standing there. She was dressed in her dressing gown and it was possible to make out that she wore a red nightie underneath. Mrs Sharpe said, "Logan, what is the matter?"

Logan replied, "Where your weasel husband?"

Mrs Sharpe said to him "My husband is not here. He is in London on business."

Logan became angrier and screamed at her, "Your husband tried to burn down the pub."

Then Tony's sister came down the stairs and she wore black lingerie, which left nothing to the imagination. She called down from

the stairs "My dad has done some dodgy deals, but he

wouldn't burn down the pub. He would not but lives at risk."
Logan looked over to the stairs gave her a cheeky wink and then
said,"Well, when you do see him, just remind him that I will not
sell him anything. I have already sold the pub and he will not get
his mucky, slimy hands on it." He nodded at both women before
returned to the car and drove away.

Little did Logan know, but Mr Sharpe was there. As Mrs
Sharpe closed the door, the sister came down the stairs and
looked at her dad, straight in the eyes. She then asked him, "Tell
me that you had nothing to do with this." Mr Sharpe looked at
her and said, "Go away little girl, this has nothing to do with
you." He went to his office closed the door, but it's not fully shut.
The sister stood outside the door and listened, in she could just
make out what her dad said on the phone. "I need these deals to
go through. The club needs to fail. I don't care how you do it,
people need to stop talking about Dorkchester.I don't care what
you have to pay, but let's take out some of the players, if they
can't fill a team they'll have to forfeit the match. This is my
town." As Mr Sharpe came out of the office, his daughter quickly
ran upstairs before he knew she was there.

"The magic of the FA cup is still going strong, we have the club
that, at the start of season, nobody had heard of, A town of about
a thousand people and a lot of those are factory workers in the
local biscuit factory. For those who don't know the story of
Dorkchester, the founder and owner of the biscuit factory decided
to keep his worker morale up so he also built the Dorkchester
stadium. This is how the club was formed. It has not had much
reason for celebration in the team's history, they have lost more
matches than they have won. They make good biscuits there but
not much else has come from the town of Dorkchester. They are

going to face the premier league superstars of Everton. Sit back as the town, and the football neutral, cheer the town of Dorkchester."

"Yes, this just shows the true beauty of the FA cup and what makes it so magical, Now the bookies have Everton as strong favourites but seeing what the Dorkchester and their manager have already pulled off, by some miracle. Logan was once one of the world's greatest players but after he had career changing injury, he fell off the face of the earth and the world had forgotten about him, until he turned up at Dorchester as the manager.He has guided them to a quarter final of the FA cup. We caught up with Tarrick, a former teammate of Logan and askedwhat he thought of the prospect of Dorkchester playing Chelsea in the semi-final if Logan can pull off another performance of dreams. This is what he had to say."

"Logan has always had an eye for the game, he could see things that other players couldn't. He reads the game so well and even in his player days, he wanted to coach. After his injury, he took it hard and did find it hard to give up the game and struggled with not having football in his life, I am so happy that he was able to find his love for football again. I would love it if Dorchester are able to pull of miracle and I'm sure Logan has some tricks up his sleeve for the Everton team. I would love to put my skills to the test against his team, but they have to get past Everton first and that is no easy task, but secretly, and don't tell anyone, but I rooting for Dorkchester., I must compliment the ground staff, considering this is a non-league club, the pitch yes, is a little ragged, but there does seem to be a good service and it isn't like the pitches that you would expect to see at non-league level."

"Well Tarrick. it will be our little secret and now we are

underway in the quarterfinal of the FA cup. Everton are already on the attack, they sweep the ball into the area and they get a shot on the goal, but Escobar has a safe pair of hands and that was early test for the non-leagues. Brooks has the ball in the middle of the field, he then feeds the ball to Rodgers and he puts in the cross into the box and it is headed away and Everton are now running up the field and Champman puts in a stern tackle and then plays ball up field. Smith is just on the edge of the box and he is taken down by a player. The referee has blown for free kick. Everton are lining up their wall. How many teams have a player laying on the floor behind the wall. Champman has come up from the centre of defence, he places the ball down on the ground and it looks like Champman is going take the free kick. He has taken a run, he hits the ball. Oh my, he has hit it along the floor and it has gone straight into the chest of the player that was lying on the floor, Oh my, he is wincing as the ball struck him straight in his chest the ball rolls out and Everton now come away with the ball and it has been played forward and they have another shot at Escobar, but it was quite as soft shot and didn't trouble the Dorkchester keeper. The ball is loose in the midfield and it is again picked up by Brooks, who passes it to Angelos and now it's put into to Tim Penfold, one of the twins, and he now gets it to his brother Calvin He now puts the ball to McFadden, who tries a shot but it goes over the bar. The Everton keeper kicks out, the ball reaches their midfield and they are making a run in the box and what a tackle from Elliot, he now gets it to Wise who is running past the defenders and he plays it to Smith and he is holding the ball up and he is taken out by the Everton defence, another free kick for Dorkchester, The Everton defence are putting up their wall and they again have a player just laying behind the wall, Champman is laying down the ball and he takes another shot, again it was full force and it has gone under the wall and gone straight into the chest of the player on the ground. He is rolling around on the ground, clutching his stomach, it looks like that one hurt. He is checked over by the physio, he has just rolled up his shirt and you can see the redness where the ball hit him, ouch. The ball went out for a throw, after rebounding off him, but Dorkchester were not able to anything with the ball and Everton clear the ball away as the referee brings the half to an end. Everton have had a couple of shots but nothing of real note and we have seen two power shots that have hit two players in the chest. If Dorkchester get any free kicks in the second half, I can't see anyone volunteer to be the one that lays down. With the power that Champman's power, if he was able to get that on target the keeper would be tested."

"We are back for the second half. Everton and Dorkchester are still locked at nil nil. Just as the second half starts rain is coming down and the little, old pitch is starting to show it wear and tear and the players are sliding as the pitch is becomes a little boggy. I don't think this club has good drainage. The Everton manager is berating the fourth official as to why this match is still being played. Everton did ask if the game should have been moved to their ground for such an important match, but the FA refused and said Dorkchester were able to host the match. We have seen some very powerful free kicks from the Dorkchester player, Champman and Everton have not been able to get a foothold in the game, we are back underway. Everton are on the attack Eliot gets a good tackle in and he feeds the ball up to Brooks, who then plays it Rodgers but he is stopped by the Everton midfielder who plays the ball on the left but Wise is there intercept. Wise plays it back up to Rodgers but Everton are there again and they get the ball forward but Tim Penfold is there to pick up the pieces and he plays it up to his brother, who brings the ball to midfielder Angelos, who plays it up to McFadden but the defenders take it off his feet and they play it up to their striker, who is now on one with the keeper, but the keeper is out quickly and takes the ball from his feet, we are in a game of tennis at the moment the ball is going back and forth between both teams, It looks like Dorkchester are going to make some changes, they are brining on their two youngsters, they are bringing Hughes and Paige. Both of these have shown ability when they have played before. Maybe Logan feels the midfield needs a little more skill. The changes have been made, Brooks and Angelos both went off and now the centre of midfield is younger but these two players are a bit more technical. Will they be able to unlock the Everton defence? Hughes is straight into the action, he has the ball and passes it to Paige and now Smith has the ball on edge of the area. Oh my, he is taken out by an Everton defender, the player is booked for the tackle. The Everton team are lining up their wall but there is a bit of shoving between the players, as they are arguing as to who should be the player who is going to lay behind the wall. It looks like they are not going to have a player on the ground, Everton line up the wall. Champman is setting up the ball and he takes the shot. Oh my. the wall did not move but Champman has just played it straight over the wall and it has gone blazing straight in the back of the net. The keeper had no chance to save it, Champman has hit a bullet of a shot, no wonder they call him the Tank. The Dorkchester all surround Champman, as he has just hit a wonder free kick. Everton, the premier league team, are now one nil down to the non-leaguer Dorkchester. The beauty of the FA cup is still going, the team that has surprised everyone this season are leading against premier league Everton. Will Everton have the answer to try and salvage this game.

Everton are trying to break down the Dorkchester defence but Champman, the player who scored that blistering free kick, is now in his familiar role at the heart of the defence. Everton have made three changes. all attacking players, they are throwing everything they can now at Dorkchester, Dorkchester are bringing on Brett Smith, I am told he is no relation to the Harvey Smith, who is already on the pitch unlike the Penfold twins, Rodgers is off. In favour ofBrett Smith.Everton are on the run with the ball, they now play it down the wing, a cross is played in but there is nobody in the box and the keeper is able to get the ball clear. It's all Everton now attack after attack, but they are not really testing the keeper,

We are reaching the final minutes of the match. Please someone pinch me. Am I dreaming? The small club from the town of Dorkchester, are on the verge of the FA cup semi-final and a trip to Wembley, for the first time in the club's history. This is why we love football, anything can happen in this game. No one saw how a town of thousand people could possible beat the team from Liverpool. Everton have one final chance as they have a corner, they have sent their keeper up to try and help to bring this level. The corner is played in, Elliot gets the ball out and now Hughes has the ball, he is running with it, he has reached the centre circle, there is no keeper and he had just taken the shot from the halfway line. The Everton keeper and players are trying to chase the ball to stop it from hitting the back of net, but they are just not fast enough and the ball has rolled into the back of the net. Yes you heard it Dorkchester are two nil up, There is a lot of arguing between the Everton players as they have conceded two goals to non-league opposition. The ref brings the match to an end and the fans are invading the pitch, they are hugging the players, who are in teardrop. They are going to be playing

Chelsea at Wembley in the semi-final of the FA cup, yes, you heard, me non-league Dorkchester are in a semi-finals of the FA cup, the greatest cup competition in the world. The question that everyone is asking, can they now go all the way to the final of the cup and dare I say win it. Only in FIFA game could this happen, but now it could happen for real. Well, I am looking forward to that match. The Chelsea superstars against the part timers. The Everton manager is arguing with the referee he feels that the game should have been called off and Dorkchester were given an advantage with the rain and the state of the pitch."

A few days after the quarterfinal, the team and their families meet in the café. They planned to release an FA Cup song for the semi-final like clubs used to when they reached the final. Angelos is organised the team and had written song, There were loads of photos, from the town's history, laid out on the table as to which ones they would to use in the video.

Logan was looking through a bunch of photos, when Lucy came and asked him how he had been. Logan was distracted, as had he found a photo of the lady who was with him on the train with him. He smiled and he turned to Lucy and asked her "Do you know this woman?

Lucy looked at the photo, saw the woman and replied, with "Yes that is Aunt Vera, she was the hub of this town. She was the town mayor at one point. She loved this town and would do anything for it, she had a special connection with the town." Logan looked at her puzzled and said, "What do you mean, she used to?" She replied, with, "She passed away many years ago, but say that same she still is watching over the town." Logan said, "But that can't be true, I met her on the train and she talked to me and I told her about my life and my journey." Lucy grabbed him by the hand and said for him to follow her. They left the café and walked up to the church, she took him up to a couple of graves and she showed him the headstone. Logan read the gravestone, 'Here lays Aunt Vera, the heart and soul of the town'. Logan wiped the tears away from his eyes and kneeled on to the ground and spoke to the grave. "I don't believe in ghosts, but if your spirit did come and speak to me and save me, I would like to thank you. This town has done so much for me and I have never felt happy until now." He got up and followed Lucy back to the café, where they were still trying to sort out all the preparation for their song.

Angelos came in, dressed in his stage outfit,

"Okay boys, let's get the show on the road." He said to everyone. The song started with him singing and all the other players as his backup singers,

"We are Dorkchester. We are Dorkchester. We are your butchers. We are your bakers.

We are Dorkchester. We are Dorkchester. We are your agents we are your plumbers.

We are Dorkchester. We are Dorkchester we are your chef we are your teachers.

We are Dorkchester. We are Dorkchester we are your factory workers. We are your bus drivers and let's not forget, we are your wrestlers."

The camera panned round the room, the player's families and friends chanted: We are Dorkchester. We are Dorkchester.

The song is played on the local radio daily and it made the national news as well.

The club had a few league matches to get through before the cup match. It was during the league match that Angelos and Brooks both were tackled badly and both suffered injuries. This meant that they would miss the cup match. The club were struggled to fill the squad, they couldn't afford to suffer anymore injuries. It was during one training session when Mary ran onto the field and screamed, "Stop! I need to say something to you." Logan and the players turned to her, well it's not every day you see a girl in high heels running on to the training field screaming. Logan said, "What do you need to tell us?" Mary looked up at them, but she stumbled and Rodgers jumped to her aid and caught her before she fell to the ground. She looked up at him and smiled and she said to him, "My hero, you have a good, safe pair of hands."

Logan was a little suspicious and said to her, "So tell us what you have come here to say." She got her balance and said, "Okay. It's my dad, he has put a hit on the players, he plans to injure as many as he can, so that you're not able to fulfil the cup match." Logan then said, "Why should we trust you and more to the point, why are you telling us?"

Mary then said, "Okay, I will be straight with you, I don't want anything to happen to my Rodgy Poo." The whole team all burst out laughing at hearing Rodgy Poo., Rodgers then said, "What are you trying say?" Mary turned and faced Rodgers directly and she told him "Look you stupid galar, I have been in love with you since the first day you came round with Tony. I have missed seeing you now that you and he are no longer hanging out. I have been waiting what seems like forever for you to ask me out. Why do you think I spent so much time with you and Tony and flirted and joke with you all the time? I don't want you to get hurt because of some silly old soccer match."

Rodgers then turned to her and replied, with "I have been in love with you too. I watch all your tik tock, videos. I am subscriber to your OF, I never felt that I would ever be good enough for you." Mary stopped him talking and with a kiss his lips. The team all cheered and applauded them. Logan then huddled the team together and said, "Okay team, we are going to have to watch ourselves out there in our next matches up to the semi-final or we are not going to be able fulfil are commitments." Even with though they are aware that opposition players were trying to injure them, Calvin Penfold was another player who was injured and would miss the semi-final. Logan was now struggling to name a team. He and Bob were in the office until late into the night trying to figure out what to do, when Mr Smith, Harvey's dad, came in and said, "Good evening gentleman" He handed them some paperwork and he said to them that Harvey had told them about their injury crisis and he would like to offer his services as reserve keeper, he could just fill a place on the bench. Hewould do everything he could for the town to make sure the match goes ahead. It was the least he could do. Logan turned to Bob and says "Hmm, that gives me an idea."

A couple days in before the semi-final, Logan had arranged to go on a date with Lucy, but Logan didn't know that on the morning of their date, Tony had been in the pub and had been spoken to Lucy,

"Lucy, good morning. You are looking well."

Lucy replied whilst pouring him a beer, "I'm doing okay."

Tony went on to say: "I know things between us didn't work out."

Lucy laughed as Tony carried on, "But I would like to think of you as a friend and wouldn't want you to get hurt. I have heard rumours that you are dating Logan,"

Lucy nodded, Tony continued, "I just want to warn you as your friend, your Logan isn't the perfect guy that he makes himself to be. I have already too much I should go." He turned to go, but Lucy grabbed his arm and said,

"If you have something to say, then say it." He then told her, "Well, seeing as you asked, I'm just reminding you that I am telling you this as a friend. Well to start with, this pub that you love so much, has been sold to developer. The developers are going to tear it down. My dad has tried to buy the pub with numerous offers, even more that it is worth. Because my dad cares about the pub." Lucy then butts in, "You are lying! Logan has said that he loves the pub, he wouldn't do that."

Tony then pulled out some paperwork and laid it on top of the bar. Lucy looked at it, they were blueprints for flats on the site of the pub. Lucy saw, at the bottom, Logan name on prints and had been signed by him. Lucy shook her head and said, "This isn't true, I don't believe you."

Tony then said, "Wait, this isn't the worst of it." He then laid out photos of Logan and a woman kissing him on the cheek. Lucy asked Tony, "Why are you showing me these pictures?" Tony grinned and said, "The woman in the picture is a hooker, a dirty little whore." He then pulled some more photos and these were of the girl kissing Logan and these pictures were of her posing naked and in sexy lingerie. Lucy then pushed the photos off the counter and shouted at him to take them away. Tony went to her and gave her a hug, he then tried to kiss her on the lips, but she pushed him away and shouted, "Go away and just leave me alone." Tony backed off and he left the pub. Lucy dropped to the floor crying. Her phone goes pinged, she has a message from Logan. It said he was looking forward to their date. Lucy was still crying whilst she sent a message to him saying: 'I can't go out with you. I'm getting back with Tony. Just delete my number and never speak to me again goodbye.'

It was the morning of the cup match and the coach was at the stadium, the whole town was there to see them off, apart from Lucy. Logan went to Captain Rodgers and handed him an envelope as he knew that the captain was, unfortunately, not going to the game as he had drawn the short straw and had to stay back to police the town. Logan asked him if he would pass on Lucy's birthday card. He had tried to ring her, but she hadn't returned his calls. He knew that something he had done seemed to have upset her somehow. Captain Rodgers said he would go and see her once they had left. He tapped Logan on his shoulder and said to him to have a good game. The players boarded the bus, the town and the families waved goodbye but just as Logan boarded, Rex came up to him he and gave him a teddy, McFadden said to Logan, "This is Rex's favourite teddy, he wants you to have it for good luck" Logan said that he would take good care of it. Brett sat on the bus when he saw some familiar faces. He jumped off the bus and ran over to them, it was his wife and children. They were all crying. Brett's wife then said to him, "I know you didn't mean to hit me, I still love you, your family still needs you." Brett tried to wipe away the tears, he knelt down and looked at his children, kissed them both on the head and hugged them. He then looked up at his wife and told her that he had been seeing someone who is helping him with his issues. She pulled him up from his knees and kissed him and said, "Go and win the match, then come home and we can be a family again." He boarded the bus, overcome with emotion. The bus drove off and the town waved them off showing of their banners of support.

Once the coach had left, Captain Rodgers went to the pub to see Lucy. She was cleaning the pub as it was completely empty, as the whole town were on the way to Wembley to watch the match. The captain said to Lucy,

"Morning Lucy you not going to match today?"

226

Lucy replied "No, not feeling up to it, I am just getting the pub ready for if they win or lose."

Captain Rodgers handed Lucy the card and told her that Logan had asked him to give it to her. She took the card and threw it on the counter and said that she didn't want anything from him. The captain then said, "Hey Lucy, I don't know what has gone on between you two but Logan is a good kid. Yes, he has made some mistakes in his past, but who hasn't."

Lucy threw some pictures on the counter and shouted "But he is still making the mistakes. I have pictures of him and a fucking slut." Captain Rodgers looked at the photos and said, "Pictures are not always what they seem to be and can be misleading. I know who the woman is and yes, she was a prostitute, but after she and Cesar got married, she gave it up to be with him and this photo, and I know this for sure as I was there, is the day of their wedding and she was kissing Logan to thank him for getting her out of that life and helping her find her true love."

Lucy then snapped back and said, "That's not the only thing I am pissed of about. He has sold the pub and they are going to turn it into houses - my pub."

Captain Rodgers looked puzzled and said, "Are you sure about that? Maybe you should read the card." Lucy picked up the card from the counter and said, "Fine." She opened it up and a sheet of paper fell to the floor. Lucy bent down and picked it up, she then said "Oh shit, I have made a huge mistake. What have I done? I have pushed away the one I love?" The captain smiled at her, and told her "It isn't too late for you to tell him how you feel I have a friend who owes me a favour and you shall go to the match."

227

"I would like to welcome you to all Wembley. What a match we have in store for you. The true wonders of the FA cup and the true beauty of the cup. We have even had an old fashioned cup song, in the past clubs would bring out a song when they got to a cup final but Dorkchester released one for the semi and currently, I'm told by my sources, it is at thirty nine in the charts. Now Dorkchester, the lowest ranked team in England is facing off against Chelsea. We have champion league winners going against shop workers in a match to get in the final. I don't know about you but I am on the edge of my seat knowing we could be on the brink of a miracle. I have heard that Hollywood are very interested in making a movie about the whole journey and the rise of Dorkchester. I think they are looking at casting David Tennant as me in the movie. Well joking aside, we have a game that it about to get started. Dorkchester have some big news. Dorkchester, a team that have been hit by injuries have had to name a former superstar on their subs bench. We have Logan, who has register himself to play and is on the bench, this is a player that, after a serious injury and he didn't think he would play again, turned away from football. He struggled to cope with life, and his life spiralled downwards, but he seems to have rebuilt himself since being at Dorkchester. Logan, a former Chelsea player, still has friends in the Chelsea team. He and Tarrick had a very good partnership,. Logan is not the only surprise on their bench, they have also named sixty six year old Smith, he is the dad of their striker, who has come out of retirement and is the club's backup keeper, as due to their injury, they did not have enough players. so he has come out of retirement. Whether he gets onto the pitch is another story. There is also an added incentive for Logan, as Hands is the player that caused the injury that changed Logan life, is now in the Chelsea team, so if Logan does end up on the field, how will he react to being face to face with him? Well let's get down to pitch side as we get the game underway,

Dorkchester have just kicked off and we are underway. Brett plays the ball to Hughes, it is a poor pass and Chelsea pick up the loose ball, they play the ball down the wing and Hands has it. He cuts across the Dorkchester defence and lifts it over, and Tarrick gets a shot, Escobar got a hand to it but Chelsea have put the ball into the back of the net. Chelsea are now one nil up. It has been all Chelsea in the opening start of this match, it looks like the dream is finally going to come to end, but what a story it has been and we have been there for every step. Chelsea have picked the ball and are on the attack. Tarrick hits a thirty yard shot and just it goes wide of the post. Hands has the ball, he plays a one two and is into the penalty area. He slides the ball into the net and now Chelsea have gone two nil up. We are looking at a landslide victory for Chelsea. The Dorkchester team have no answer for the Chelsea attack. Chelsea come again, Tarrick this time, has picked up the ball and he hits it and Escobar is just not able to stop it from going into the back of net. Chelsea are three nil up as the half comes to end. The Dorkchester players look disappointed as they troop off the field."

Logan was the last one to walk into the changing room. There was a table in the middle of the room that had bottles of water and a bowl of fruit. Logan upturned the table and the water and fruit went flying across the room, He then looked at the players and yelled, "What the Fuck was that? I can't believe what I am watching out there! Yes, they're winners and superstars but we are not here to get their autographs. We are here to show the world that we are Dorkchester and proud to be Dorkchester. Now stop fucking kissing their arses and someone put in a tackle or two and if it's not too much trouble, maybe a shot on goal. Tank, where are the tackles? You need to scare off these players, you need to show these players who the true boss is. Are you not the British heavyweight champion? Now, I only registered myself as a player due to our injuries, but I am bringing myself on for the second half. Bob is going to be in charge for the rest of the match. He will be deciding the tactics. Now I want to hear you say it: We are Dorkchester. We are Dorkchester…" The whole room began to chant 'We are Dorkchester as they headed to the pitch for the second half.

"We are back for the second half. Hold on! What is going on? There seem to be a helicopter trying to land on the centre circle. It is just hovering, the door is opening, a woman is getting out and she jumps down. The stewards are trying to stop her and trying to get her of the pitch, but Logan is walking over to her and talking to her."

Lucy got out of the helicopter and spoke to Logan. "I am sorry I shouldn't have listened to Tony. I should have known that he was lying about you and should have trusted my heart." Logan smiled and just kissed her on the lips and told her that he loved her but if she didn't mind he had a match to win.

"Well, after the little intermission before, now we get the second half underway and after time away from the game, Logan, one of the world's greatest players, having played for some biggest teams in Europe, now he is playing for Dorkchester. We are unsure if he can still play, no one has seen him kick a ball for almost two years since his injury in the world cup final. Can he help Dorkchester in getting a consolation goal in this match? The team who have shown the true meaning of the cup, they have shown the true magic of the cup. With Chelsea three nil up, the ref gets the second half underway. Logan has the ball, oh my, he is weaving in between the Chelsea players he has just nutmegged Tarrick, a former teammate. He plays a one to one with McFadden and he now he is one on one with the keeper, he slides the ball into the back of the net. What a goal! That was setup and scored by Logan himself, it seems that he has not lost his spark. Chelsea have the ball again, they are on their way up the field and what a tackle by Champman. He gets the ball up to the midfield to Brooks, who finds Smith, he plays it to McFadden. Chelsea intercept the ball and play it out. Logan picks up the loose ball and he has just a thirty yard shot and if I didn't witness it, I would not believe it, but Dorkchester have brought the game to three two. Surely they can't get back in this game but the way this team have come out in the second half with Logan on the ball, anything could happen, Chelsea have the ball, Hands plays it Tarrick who is now running on goal. Bam, he has just run into the Champman. It's like he has run straight into a brick wall. Champman plays the ball up, with a long seeking pass. It is picked up by Smith, he plays a soft shot on the keeper. Dorkchester have picked up the ball as it's loose in the defence. Brooks plays a pass to Logan. He plays a defence, cutting pass and McFadden is now on the ball, he has chipped the ball over the keeper. Oh my, the comeback is on, the lowest team in the cup, have just drawn level and the way this match is playing out, I can see Dorkchester winning. The whole town of Dorkchester is here to witness this achievement and how this team are making miracles. This is such a powerful story, the minnows have pegged the mighty Chelsea back. We are reaching the eighty sixth minute of this semi-final of the FA cup match between Dorkchester and Chelsea. Yes, if I wasn't commentating on and watching this, I would say that this was some sort of dream, Chelsea have a corner, the ball is swung in and Tarrick jumps in the air and he gets a head on the ball and he diverts it past the Keeper and Chelsea now lead four three in the dying minutes of this match.

231

The Dorkchester players look so defeated, they have given their all. The ref has checked his watch, the whistle is up to his lips and there we have it. Chelsea will be going into the cup final but they have been in a match here today. The Dorkchester players have dropped to their knees. The town should be proud of every player, they have shown that the FA cup is the greatest competition in the world. How the smallest team can take on the super powers. The Chelsea players are pulling the Dorkchester players to their feet and hugging them. It looks like they are forming a guard of honour to show their respect for the Dorkchester players. The whole stadium is on their feet applauding and cheering. Even the Chelsea fans are applauding the Dorkchester players. Just listen to that roar of WE ARE DORKCHESTER. WE ARE DORKCHESTER. Every fan, steward, even the press are chanting the Dorkchester name. The young lady that came out of the helicopter has her hands around Logan and is kissing him as they walk off the pitch, Well I don't know about you, but today I have seen probably the greatest match in the history of football, you have got to love it! Well until next time, good evening."

The Dorkchester and Chelsea players swapped shirts and chatted in the tunnel. Tarrick and Hands came over to Logan and Lucy and Hands said, "Logan, great game out there today, I just want to say that I am so sorry for my tackle in the world cup I didn't."

Logan stopped him from saying anything else and replied, "It is okay, these things happen in football and if it wasn't for that tackle, I would have never found love."

Logan hugged Hands and asked if he they could swap shirts. Then Tarrick said to Logan, "Well buddy, you had us on the ropes out there today, I am so happy for you and it looks like you have got your groove back. Maybe I can have a word and see if we can get you back into the big time." Logan responded, "I appreciate the offer, but I think I am going to stay at Dorchester. There is a lovely bar owner that I would like to ask to marry me." Lucy blurted out, "Pardon, what did you say?" and before Lucy could say anything else and in front the Wembley Tunnel, Logan got on his knees and he was passed the captain's armband by Brooks and he then asked Lucy, holding out the captain's armband, "Lucy, will you marry me?" Lucy didn't need to think about it and within seconds she said yes. Logan placed the captain's armband on Lucy's arm as they kissed and the tunnel erupted in cheers.

The End

PS
You are probably wondering what happened to the team after the semi final game and the future of Dorkchester FC. The Club, after it's FA exploits was saved, as the biscuit factory was bought by investors, who also bought into the club and turned their FA cup journey into a Hollywood blockbuster. It was even nominated for an Oscar. As for the players, well:

GK
Raul Escobar he continues to play in goal. Logan, with the help of some lawyers, helped him to register as a doctor in the UK and he is now the town's doctor. He was also able to bring his family over to the UK and they are happily reunited.

LB
Luke Wise is still playing for the club, He has also opened a chain of restaurants and appeared and won MasterChef.

CB
Tom Elliot is still leading the defence and after his dad's retirement is running the clothes shop.

CB
Charles Champman (The Tank) retired from football after the FA cup season and moved to America in order to fulfil his dream of

being a wrestler. He is currently an impact wrestling superstar.

RB

Tim Penfold is still the playing for the club and he is still enjoying being a baker. He and his wife are expecting their first child.

RM

Calvin Penfold like his brother he continues to play for the club and he and his partner are also expecting a baby. It looks like the next generation of Penfolds will be taking over the family's businesses. The Penfolds will be a part of the Dorkchester town for many years.

CM

Augustus Brooks continues to play and sell houses although he never did sell the pub or the cottage.

CM

Mateo Angelos no longer plays football. After he was given the opportunity to appear on Drag Race, he was offered his own chat show. He now again will plays for a pub team but he and his wife are enjoying being celebrities.

LM

Rover Rodger continues to play for the club. He also passed out from the College of Policing and he polices the town alongside his dad.

David McFadden is still scoring goals in front of his son and they have recently started a charity called Austin Football. He also continues to be the town plumber.

CF

Harvey Smith was signed for Watford after he was seen by a scout and he is currently banging in the goals in the premier League, not bad for the son of a factory worker.

CB

Cesar is still playing for the club. He also married the hooker who pretended to be engaged to him so he didn't get deported, they fell in love and she now no longer works on the streets and they are happily married.

CM

Brett has retired from football but he has moved back in with his family, he is seeing a therapist to help with his grief from his days in the army.

CDM

Stephen Glass continues to be the Head teacher of the school and plays for the club and he has also recently written a book called the Gay Footballer.

CF

Terry Hughes was signed by Chelsea and is a part of their youth team, after Logan recommended him to the club.

CF

Sam Paige was signed by Leeds and he is a part of their youth team and he played and scored on his premier league debut. His dad came around to the fact he would not have been a good doctor and is proud that he found his true calling.

Bob Continues to coach the club and drive the busses.

Logan continues to play and manage the club and he married Lucy. They are also expecting their first child. Logan turned down numerous offers from a host of clubs wanting to sign him but he told them he was happy at Dorkchester and his love of the game continues.

You are also probably wondering what happen to Tony. Well, after his dad was arrested for fraud, Tony had his contract terminated at Foxford and he has struggled to find a club that would take him on. The last I heard he was stacking shelves at a supermarket.

The End